# Golf
## A Very
## Peculiar
## History ™

With NO added bogeys

'A golf course outside a big town serves an excellent purpose in that it segregates, as though a concentration camp, all the idle and idiot well-to-do.'

Osbert Sitwell

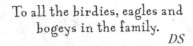

To all the birdies, eagles and
bogeys in the family.
*DS*

Editor: Jamie Pitman

Artists: Mark Bergin, David Antram

Published in Great Britain in MMXI by
Book House, an imprint of
**The Salariya Book Company Ltd**
25 Marlborough Place, Brighton BN1 1UB
**www.salariya.com**
**www.book-house.co.uk**

HB ISBN-13: 978-1-907184-75-8

© The Salariya Book Company Ltd MMXI

3 5 7 9 8 6 4
A CIP catalogue record for this book is available
from the British Library.
Printed and bound in China.
Printed on paper from sustainable sources.
Reprinted MMXIV.

Visit our website at **www.book-house.co.uk**
or go to **www.salariya.com**
for **free** electronic versions of:
**You Wouldn't Want to be an Egyptian Mummy!**
**You Wouldn't Want to be a Roman Gladiator!**
**You Wouldn't Want to Join Shackleton's Polar Expedition!**
**You Wouldn't Want to Sail on a 19th-Century Whaling Ship!**

# Golf
## A Very
## Peculiar
## History™

With NO added bogeys

Written by
**David Arscott**

Created and designed by
**David Salariya**

BOOK HOUSE
a SALARIYA imprint

'Some of us worship in churches, some in synagogues, some on golf courses.'

Adlai Stevenson, US politician

'The only time my prayers are never answered is on the golf course.'

Billy Graham, evangelist

'They say that golf is like life, but don't believe them. Golf is more complicated than that.'

Gardner Dickinson, professional golfer

'Golf is an open exhibition of overweening ambition, courage deflated by stupidity, skill soured by a whiff of arrogance.'

Alistair Cooke, writer and broadcaster

'If profanity had an influence on the flight of the ball, the game of golf would be played far better than it is.'

Horace G. Hutchinson, golfing author

# Contents

# A few reasons to play golf

- A walk of about five miles over 18 holes is excellent heart-and-lung exercise which burns up hundreds of calories and reduces your bad cholesterol.

- You'll be out in the fresh air in attractive scenery, with a breeze in your face and clean air in your lungs.

- It's a retreat from the dull cares of life, which miraculously fall away the moment you step on to that first tee.

- The achievement of hitting a perfect shot and watching your ball drop into the hole will live with you for days to come.

- You can start playing the game at any age, and, with the luck of good health, can carry on playing it for life.

- You'll meet people you didn't know before, making new friends and valuable business acquaintances.

- It's character-building, teaching you to take the rough with the smooth, to play honourably and to show a brave face in adversity.

# A few reasons not to play golf

- Lugging a heavy bag full of clubs over your shoulder for hours at a time can play havoc with your tendons – and that's before you damage them with your golf swing.

- Rain, sleet and hail are bad enough to walk in without having to whack a tiny ball into a howling gale at the same time.

- It takes but a couple of strokes to remind you why your handicap is as poor as it is – and why your life in general is a mess.

- For every good shot there are ten bad ones – and it's the worst of them you wake up thinking about at four in the morning.

- Once you've mastered the rudiments of the game, you know you'll get steadily worse at it with every advancing year.

- Just imagine having to put up with the endless carping, cheating and uncalled-for advice of complete strangers!

- As plain failure gives way to abject humiliation you'll end up either wanting to throttle your opponent or to bury your head in a bunker.

A 12th Century game of golf? An illustration from Bede's *Life of St Cuthbert*, showing ball games and a raised stick.

# TEEING Off

**P**ut a rolling object in front of a man and he'll kick it. Give him a stick and he'll thwack it. (Many women have this primitive urge, too.) This means that, quite unknown to themselves, our ancestors were yearning to play golf the moment they emerged from their caves into a landscape of weather-rounded rocks and fallen branches.

Why did they take so long about it? Because, as any genuine golfer will tell you, the sport is one of the pinnacles of civilisation, and – in common with our other illustrious arts and sciences – its sublime subtleties and perplexing profundities could only be developed over a long period of time.

Purists love a good argument about when golf really started. In the 12th century *Life of St Cuthbert* by the English monk St Bede there's an illustration (*see page 8*) of a man about to strike a ball with what looks pretty much like a crude golf club, and in a stained-glass window in Gloucester Cathedral, dating from around 1350 (*below*), a club-wielding figure is surely aiming to take a swipe at the small ball in front of him.

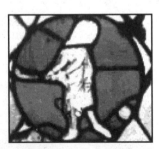

Golfer in stained glass window reveals Gloucester Cathedral's sporting past?

# But is it golf?

- **Italy** – The Romans played 'paganica', using curved sticks to hit feather-stuffed leather balls not unlike early golf balls. We don't know the rules, so it may have been a form of hockey.

- **Persia** – In 'chaugun' the players used a mallet to hit the ball, but the game sounds much closer to polo, with the players mounted on horses.

- **France** – The game called 'jeu de mail' originated in the 15th century. The ball was driven through hoops with a mallet – making it a forerunner of croquet rather than golf.

- **China** – From the 8th to the 14th centuries the social elite played 'Chuiwan', the word being a composite of 'hitting' and 'small ball', and there are illustrations of it in the Palace Museum in Beijing. The balls were knocked into holes, as in golf, and the rules seem to have been similar.

- **The Netherlands** – Is it a coincidence that the game known as 'colf', a craze over there in medieval times, sounds so much like 'golf'? The Dutch don't think so. They didn't hit the ball into holes, but a Latin manual published in Antwerp in 1552 includes remarks by colf players which echo those you can hear on any golf course today: 'You wait your turn'; 'Step back a bit, you're in my light'; and 'I didn't play badly – it just wasn't my day'.

## Missing links

What's lacking in all of the examples on page 11, however, is the idea that golf should be played out in the countryside over long distances – the very essence of the experience, after all.

That's why we prefer the story, daft as it is, that the sport originated with Scottish shepherds who, in their idle moments, upturned their crooks and used them to pitch pebbles into rabbit holes in the rugged coastal landscape around St Andrews.

The attraction of this theory is that it chimes so well with two undeniable facts – that the game as we know it today was developed in Scotland and that St Andrews, on the country's chilly North Sea coast in Fife, would become the cradle of modern golf.

## Too much of a good thing

Although golf was probably played at St Andrews even before the founding of the famous university there in 1411, the earliest surviving written record of the game in Scotland dates from 1457, when parliament ruled that, along with football, it was to be 'utterly cryed down and not to be used'. It had already become so popular that young men were neglecting a vital duty. They would rather be (surprise, surprise!) stroking golf balls into holes than practising the archery skills they needed to fight 'the auld enemy', England – with whom the Scots were regularly at war. The problem clearly didn't go away, because this ban on playing golf became a bit of a habit, being reaffirmed in 1470 and again in 1491. We have to imagine the young bloods of the day enjoying their game wherever they could find a useful space for it, and that almost certainly included churchyards in the towns. This must have been provocation enough for the ministers of the 'kirk', but even worse was the fact that a passion for golf was seducing players from their Sunday worship.

In 1596 a goldsmith, Walter Hay, was brought before the authorities at Elgin for 'playing at the boulis and golff upoun Sundaye in the tyme of the sermon' and had to promise, under the threat of a fine, never to do it again at any time on the Lord's Day.

St Andrews, as you might expect, was a hotbed of golfing resistance, and the church grew so weary of dealing with the offenders that in 1599 it drew up a scale of punishments, ranging from cash fines to public repentance and 'depravation fra their offices' – the sack.

Golf devotees continued in their sinful ways, though. In 1651 five East Lothian men were 'ordained to make their public repentance', and one of them lost his job as a deacon.

Up in Aberdeen, meanwhile, another insult to the church was perpetrated by the bookbinder John Allen. In 1613 he was convicted 'for setting ane goiff ball in the kirk yeard, and striking the same against the kirk'. We don't know whether this was as the result of a bad shot or whether the door was his target.

## The sport of kings

The Scottish golfing craze wasn't confined to the man in the street. A succession of monarchs fell in love with the game, which must have helped improve its standing among the upper classes and encouraged its spread throughout the land. Here are a few of them.

**James IV**
Only 15 when he came to throne in 1488, James made a peace treaty with the English four years later, and the defence of the realm suddenly wasn't quite such an important issue – parliament's ban on playing golf could be relaxed.

It would of course be far-fetched to suggest that James signed the Treaty of Perpetual Peace (some hopes!) with Henry VII purely to give him free rein on the links, but he did throw himself into it with huge enthusiasm. Golf was all the rage!

The Lord High Treasurer's accounts for 1503 show the king not only buying clubs and balls (they were very expensive), but shelling out three French crowns 'to play at the golf with the Earl of Bothwell' – which seems to imply that he wagered money on the match and ended up losing. James may even have helped promote the game in England. As part of the deal with the English he married Margaret, Henry's daughter, and ten years later we find Katharine of Aragon, Henry VIII's queen, writing to Cardinal Wolsey that all the king's subjects were 'very glad, I thank God, to be busy at the golf'.

## Royal golf courses

More than 60 golf clubs throughout the world have the right to include 'Royal' in their names, because of the kings and queens who have patronised them.

William IV first set the ball rolling, granting the honour to the Royal Perth, Scotland, in 1833, and to the Royal & Ancient at St Andrews the following year.

Outside the British Isles there are Royal clubs in Australia, Canada, the Czech Republic, India, Kenya, Malaysia, Malta, South Africa, Sri Lanka and Zimbabwe.

# Mary, Queen of Scots

Whether Mary was an early lady golfer we can't be sure, but her enemies (and she had plenty of them) certainly claimed she was.

Mary, who would later be executed for treason on the orders of her cousin, Queen Elizabeth, should have been in mourning in 1567 after her husband, Lord Darnley, was murdered. Perhaps she was, but wicked tongues put it about that she'd had a hand in his assassination and – a sure sign that she didn't care – that she'd been seen out on the golf course a few days later enjoying herself.

No dead husband's going to ruin this winning streak!

**James VI of Scotland and I of England**

He may have had to carry that awkward brace of titles around with him after he united the two thrones of Scotland and England in 1603, but the scholarly James (sponsor of the King James Bible) certainly wasn't in two minds about his golf. He appointed the Edinburgh bow-maker William Mayne royal club-maker for life and granted the patent for golf ball making in Scotland to James Melville, to 'furnische the said kingdom with better golf balls'. This was evidently a serious matter, because in his *Letters of Licence* James noted that 'no small quantity of gold and silver' was transported from Scotland every year for the import of golf balls.

Poor James Melville got himself into a spot of bother some years later, during the reign of James's son, Charles I. He claimed that his agreement with James allowed him to charge a tax on every golf ball made by anyone else, and he sent armed men into an Edinburgh workshop to seize balls from a manufacturer who had refused to pay up. Unfortunately for him the privy council refused to recognise his claim and he was given a fine.

## Charles I

Legend has it that the king received the news of the 1641 Irish Rebellion while playing golf on the Leith links, and that (like Drake at Plymouth Hoe) he finished the game before troubling himself with more tiresome matters.

Charles got himself into all sorts of scrapes before having his head lopped off in 1649. With hindsight, he would have been a happier man if he'd concentrated on his golf instead.

## The first golf international

In 1681 the Duke of York (later to become James VII and II) was staying in Scotland when he heard two English noblemen claim that golf was an English sport.

This ridiculous assertion was too much to bear, and James immediately challenged them to a golfing duel on the links at Leith. He wisely chose as his partner James Paterson, a humble cobbler but also the local golf champion.

Scotland duly beat England – and the prize money enabled Paterson to buy a substantial house in the Canongate of Edinburgh.

## Brought to Look

We get a few clues as to how golf was played in 17th-century Scotland from a Latin grammar book written for the pupils of Aberdeen Grammar School by the Master, David Wedderburn. In his *Vocabula*, first published in 1636, he gives words, phrases and complete sentences the boys might expect to use in a variety of areas – including golf, which he named 'baculus', or club.

As he includes words for holes and bunkers, refers to uphill and downhill strokes and mentions teeing off on sand, it's clear that the lads were playing around the dunes on the coastal links. They were already using different clubs for different types of strokes.

Here are a few of his terms for the equipment:

**Baculus fereus** – an iron-headed club described as a 'bunkard club', presumably for lofting balls out of a bunker
**Baculi caput** – the head of the club
**Baculi caulis** – the shaft
**Pila clavaria** – the ball (literally 'a ball like a skull', because of the stitched leather)

And now a few phrases which may help confuse your playing partner at a crucial point in the game:

**Frustra es** – 'That's a miss!'
**Bene tibi cessit hic ictus** – 'That's well struck!'
**Immissa est in paludem** – 'It's in the mire!'

It was another hundred years or so before the world was entertained by the very first book completely devoted to golf – by a Scotsman, of course. Thomas Mathieson's mock-heroic poem *The Goff* was published in Edinburgh in 1743.

The poem celebrates in a humorously over-the-top manner 'the manly sport' being played on the links at Leith by a group of the Edinburgh judges, lawyers and other pillars of society.

*Macdonald and unmatch'd Dalrymple ply*
*Their pond'rous weapons, and the green defy;*
*Rattray for skill, and Corse for strength renown'd*
*Stewart and Lesly beat the sandy ground,*
*And Brown and Alson, Chiefs well known to fame,*
*And numbers more the Muse forbears to name.*

## Gentlemen golfers

Mathieson's poem was the critical point at which a hugely popular but somewhat randomly organised cross-country pursuit began to be shaped and controlled as a sport with well defined rules and etiquette – broadly the game of golf that we recognise today.

Several of the players whose virtues were trumpeted in Mathieson's poem had formed the quaintly named Company of Gentlemen Golfers, and in 1744 they decided to hold an open competition at Leith. Presumably they already had some pretty good notions about what constituted fair and unfair play, but they now drew up the first ever laws of the game.

Drop a 21st-century book of rules on your foot and you'd probably break it. This first stab at the exercise (*see pages 24–25*) was fairly basic, but the essentials are there, covering such matters as obstacles on the course, dropping a stroke for a lost ball, the order of play on the green, retrieving your ball from water ('wattery filth' was evidently a hazard at Leith), avoiding an opponent's ball and so on.

The Leith 'gentlemen' (later the Honourable Company of Edinburgh Golfers) must have been quietly satisfied to see their rules immediately adopted as the norm among Scottish golfers, although their fellow players up at St Andrews would – as the Royal & Ancient Golf Club – eventually become the official arbiters of the British game.

## Enter the Americans

Golf clubs now began to proliferate. In 1766 the Blackheath in London became the very first outside Scotland, but even more of a landmark was the founding of the South Carolina Golf Club at Charleston in the USA, the first outside Britain.

This was in 1786. Three years earlier the last shot had been fired in the American Revolution, which freed the colony from British rule. Now there began a stealthier revolution, with (in sporting terms, at least) a similar come-uppance for the Old Country.

Golf was about to become a world game – and the Americans would soon be calling the shots.

# The first Laws of the Game

The 'Articles & Laws in Playing at Golf' drawn up by the Company of Gentlemen Golfers at Leith on 7th March, 1744.

- You must Tee your Ball within a Club's length of the Hole.

- Your Tee must be upon the Ground.

- You are not to change the Ball which you Strike off the Tee.

- You are not to remove Stones, Bones or any Break Club for the sake of playing your Ball, Except upon the fair Green & that only within a Club's length of your Ball.

- If your Ball comes among Watter or any wattery filth, you are at liberty to take out your Ball & bringing it behind the hazard and Teeing it you may play it with any Club and allow your Adversary a Stroke for so getting out your Ball.

- If your Balls be found any where touching one another, You are to lift the first Ball, till you play the last.

- At Holling, you are to play your Ball honestly for the Hole, and, not to play upon your Adversary's Ball not lying in your way to the Hole.

- If you should lose your Ball, by its being taken up, or any other way, you are to go back to the Spot where you struck last, and drop another Ball, And allow your adversary a Stroke for the misfortune.

- No man at Holling his Ball, is to be allowed, to mark his way to the Hole with his Club, or anything else.

- If a Ball be stopp'd by any person, Horse, Dog, or any thing else, The Ball so stop'd must be play'd where it lyes.

- If you draw your Club in order to Strike & proceed so far in the Stroke as to be bringing down your Club; If then, your Club shall break in any way, it is to be Accounted a Stroke.

- He, whose Ball lyes farthest from the Hole is obliged to play first.

- Neither Trench, Ditch or Dyke, made for the Preservation of the Links, nor the Scholars' Holes or the Soldiers' Lines, shall be accounted a Hazard; But the Ball is to be taken out/Teed/and play'd with any Iron Club.

*John Rattray, Capt*

It was a great design, but Greg soon realised that he'd forgotten to include the fairway.

# UP HILL AND DOWN DALE

If you've never pitched a golf shot into the water or had to struggle getting the ball out of a bunker you've obviously been playing on the wrong courses. After all, anyone who longs for a smooth, obstacle-free surface should really be playing billiards. What brings nobility to golf is the constant striving to overcome adversity. A glance at those first rules drawn up in Leith back in 1744 shows that the players had not only 'wattery filth' to contend with, but further hazards such as dogs, horses, stones and bones. Today's course designers have to resort to other kinds of torment.

## Rough and tough

You'll sometimes hear the uninstructed refer to all courses as 'links', but the word properly applies only to those by the sea which share the conditions our gentlemen golfers first experienced at Leith and St Andrews. These doughty pioneers happily tackled a tousled terrain of sand and scrub horribly unsuited to displays of perfection. There are still plenty of courses like this in Scotland, England and Ireland (the Open Championship is always played on them), and some golfers take an almost spiritual pleasure in their stark simplicity. Forget the veritable army of maintenance staff you find mowing, trimming and watering the more elaborate inland courses: sheep will often keep the grass down here, just as they did in days gone by.

Many of the links have an 'outward' nine holes in one direction along the coast followed by an 'inward' nine in the other direction, and this demands great skill in adapting to a wind which beats into your face during one half of the round and whips your ball away into the distance during the other. It's a man-against-nature challenge.

Here's a links check-list:

- They're next to water, usually the sea
- The soil is sandy and drains easily
- There are few trees
- The course is open to the weather, which means that conditions are often blustery
- The fairways are uneven
- The rough includes areas thickly covered with grassy tussocks
- There are deep 'pot bunkers' – originally sand dunes hollowed out by sheltering sheep

# Why 18 holes?

The number of holes on early golf courses varied from as few as 5 to as many as 24, and 18 became the norm only in 1858. Some garrulous old codger in the clubhouse bar is bound to relate the yarn that Scottish players paused to swig a shot of whisky at each hole, and that there were exactly 18 shots in their 'fifth' bottle – a fifth of a gallon that is. We're sorry to scotch a good story, but the influential Royal & Ancient fixed the course at 18 holes when they reorganised their Old Course at St Andrews to make nine holes, each played twice.

# Scotland's ten top links courses

1. **St Andrews Old Course**, Fife
2. **Royal Dornoch**, Dornoch, Sutherland
3. **Turnberry Ailsa Course**, Turnberry, Ayrshire
4. **Prestwick**, Prestwick, South Ayrshire
5. **Carnoustie**, Carnoustie, Angus
6. **Royal Troon**, Troon, South Ayrshire
7. **Muirfield**, Gullane, East Lothian
8. **Royal Aberdeen**, Aberdeen, Scotland
9. **Montrose**, Montrose, Angus
10. **Machrihanish**, Machrihanish, Mull of Kintyre

## Giving God a helping hand

When the American golfer Sam Snead first set eyes on the Old Course at St Andrews in 1946 he exploded 'Down home we plant cow beets on land like that!'

Poor Sam seems to have been the victim of a common delusion – that golf should only be played in an earthly paradise of lush meadows, sweeping lawns, deep valleys and extensive lakes, with distant vistas seen through artfully scattered stands of branchy trees.

Today's golf courses cost millions (of pounds, dollars or whatever other currency you like to spend) and the most impressive of them are undoubtedly stunningly beautiful. The 18th-century English landscape architect Capability Brown, who dug lakes and threw up hills in the grounds of the aristocracy's country houses, has at last met his match in the modern golf course designer with his phalanxes of bulldozers. From its humble beginnings the golf course has become an artificial recreation of God's handiwork, with a good many improvements along the way.

# A beginner's guide to golf:
## 1. The golf course

- **Tee box or teeing ground** – Where you start, full of hope, by placing your ball on the tee peg and striking it as hard as you can.

- **The fairway** – The closely cropped area between the tee and the green. This is what you're aiming for unless you have enough power to reach the green straight away (which you haven't).

- **The rough** – The unkempt grassy areas alongside the fairway, to which your ball will be irresistibly drawn.

- **Bunkers** – Depressions filled with sand which have been deliberately designed as hazards. (As have lakes, ponds, streams etc.) Devilishly hard to get out of.

- **The apron** – An area on some courses between the fairway and the green, its grass cut to a length shorter than the first and longer than the second.

- **The green or putting green** – The manicured finishing point of the game with the hole more or less at its centre. Rolling the ball in with your putter looks like the easiest thing in the world – until you try it.

It wasn't always like that. The men who created the earliest inland courses at the beginning of the 20th century took their inspiration from the Scottish links, sensitively fitting their fairways and greens into the existing landscape. Before long, though, the urge to outsmart the Creator became irresistible. Bunkers became enormous and water featured everywhere – as lakes, streams and fountains, and even (at the Coeur d'Alene resort in the Rocky Mountains) to support the world's only floating green.

## fazio digs deep

Exhibit A in any ranking of over-the-top course creation has to be Shadow Creek, designed by the prolific Tom Fazio for the casino owner Steve Wynn in a stretch of the Nevada Desert outside Las Vegas. It opened in 1989.

Fazio's budget was vast (reportedly $40 million) and his brief absurdly demanding: he must fashion from this flat and arid wilderness a dramatic course which would include rolling hillsides, grassland, lakes, creeks, waterfalls and fast-flowing streams flowing through rocky outcrops. There were to be 21,000 pine trees in a landscape inhabited by several species of exotic birds and (a memory of the transformed desert?) Australian wallabies.

No problem! Fazio simply dug a hole 60ft deep over an area of half a square mile (so moving 2.8 million cubic yards of earth) and then imported everything he needed.

## Costing the earth

Amazing it may be, but don't expect environmentalists to approve this assault on the natural order. Golf courses are increasingly criticised for the damage they cause – spraying fertilisers and pesticides with gay abandon and investing in extensive watering regimes to keep their lakes full and their greens lushly carpeted.

It's time for some figures:

- There are about **32,000** golf courses in the world, including **17,000** in the United States and **2,500** in Britain.

- The average 18-hole golf course occupies about **150 acres** of land, half of it being maintained grass.

- The United Nations has estimated that golf clubs world-wide use **2.5 billion gallons** (**9.5 billion litres**) of water every day.

The good news is that the message is getting across – and not all clubs are set on turning deserts into parkland:

- The Coober Pedy golf course in Australia's Outback is in an area so arid that no grass grows at all. Players have to borrow a 20 cm-square piece of artificial turf from the clubhouse, before they tee off in extreme heat, often facing wind-driven dust.

- In 2010 the New Malton Golf Club in Cambridgeshire claimed to be Britain's first organic golf course. Chemical-free, and with a full-time ecologist on board, it boasted woodpeckers, kestrels, owls, pheasants and hares in its out-of-bounds areas – and had a resident stoat on its 8th hole.

- In the same year the singer Justin Timberlake set a high profile example by refashioning the Mirimichi golf course in Memphis, Tennessee, as a 'green haven'. He expanded the areas given over to wetland, wildflowers and native grasses and rigged his irrigation system to use recycled rainwater. Mirimichi became the only golf course in the world to hold certificates from both the Audubon Society and the Golf Environmental Organization.

- Some courses in the Saudi Arabian desert mix oil with the local fine sand in order to prevent it blowing away. The greens, with impeccable logic, are referred to as 'browns'.

## Highs and lows

The world's highest known course is at the Tactu Golf Club in Morococha, Peru, sitting at a lung-aching 14,335 ft (4,379 m) above sea level at its lowest point. That's just a little higher than the Yak Course at Kupup, East Sikkim in the Himalayas – 13,025 ft (3,970 m) – where snow sometimes prevents play.

The lowest lying is Furnace Creek, an 18-hole oasis course in California's parched Death Valley. At 214 ft (65 m) below sea level it presents unusual challenges, the ball being influenced by the greater gravity and barometric pressure forces.

# A beginner's guide to golf:
## 2. How to score

- **Par** – The number of strokes that a quality ('scratch' or 0 handicap) player is expected to make in order to complete a hole, a round or a tournament.

- **Bogey** – One over par. If par for a hole is 4 and you take 5 strokes you've bogeyed it – and you're doing pretty well for a beginner. Anything worse you could call a double-bogey etc, but probably you'll just say (quietly, and blushing) that you were ten over par.

- **Birdie** – One under par. (Coined at the Atlantic City Country Club in Northfield, New Jersey, in 1899 – but you don't need to know this.)

- **Eagle** – Two under par.

- **Albatross, or double eagle** – Three under par. When Gene Sarazen reached the 1935 US Masters final with one it became known as 'the shot heard around the world'.

- **Condor** – Four under par. Recorded only four times ever.

- **Ostrich** – Five under par and thought impossible. Forget it!

## Tripping up Trump

Money talks and is usually persuasive when businessmen want to build golf courses in controversial places. In 2008 (reminding everyone within earshot that his mother was a Scot), the American billionaire magnate Donald Trump announced that he was going to lavish £750 million on constructing 'the world's greatest golf course' at Menie, near Aberdeen, and would call it the Trump International Golf Links.

Two years later, having been given the green light by the Scottish government (which liked the scheme's 'economic and social benefits'), Trump found himself drawn into a confrontation with a humble salmon fisherman. Michael Forbes' land lay plumb in the middle of Trump's proposed development, and the media dubbed him 'the hero of Balmedie' when he refused to sell it. Trump was sufficiently needled to get personal, condemning the state of Forbe's land. 'Take a look and see how badly maintained that piece of property is,' he said. 'It's disgusting. There are rusty tractors, rusty oil cans. I actually asked him, "Are you doing this on purpose to try and make me look bad, so I have to pay some more money?"'

Forbes has now sold an acre of his land to a group of protesters, among them celebrities and conservationists, who called their campaign 'Tripping up Trump' – arguing that a golf centre, 10-storey hotel and hundreds of houses would ruin an ecologically sensitive dune system. The fight was on!

*What on earth would the Company of Gentlemen Golfers have had to say about it all?*

'Columbus went around the world in 1492. That isn't a lot of strokes when you consider the course.' – Lee Trevino

# CHAPTER TWO

# THE TOOLS FOR THE JOB

n 1895, the year in which the US Masters was inaugurated, the United States Golf Association banned the use of pool cues for putting. You only have to imagine how useful a well-chalked cue would be a few feet from the flag on a baize-smooth green to suspect a sadistic streak in the golfing authorities. You also realise why players, forced to wield what amounts to an upended walking stick to coax a capricious ball hundreds of yards through all kinds of terrain into a tiny hole, should be so obsessed about the finer points of the equipment at their disposal.

Watch the agony on the face of the seasoned professional. Does his position warrant a 3-iron? He consults his caddie and a 4-iron comes out of the bag. Ah no, the breeze has picked up, so perhaps a 5-iron would be better after all. On the other hand . . .

Please don't tell him to get a life. This *is* his life, and it pays him very well. The wrong choice of clubs can lose him big prize money.

## Hawthorn and ash

Those first Scottish golfers lacked this luxury of choice. One of the earliest accounts of the sport at St Andrews appears in the diary of James Melville, who was a university student there from 1569–1574. A keen golfer, he refers to his 'club and balls' – which suggests that he had but a single stick to do all the work.

It would, of course, have been made entirely of wood, although the earliest surviving clubs have the relative sophistication of a hard wood (usually hawthorn) for the heads and a more whippy, springy wood (often ash or alder) for the shafts.

# A beginner's guide to golf: 3. Your set of clubs

In competitive golf you're allowed a maximum of 14 clubs in your bag. Here's your choice:

- **Woods** – They're actually made of steel nowadays, but these are the heavyweight big hitters. The no. 1 wood is known as the 'driver', and top players use it when teeing off. The higher the number, the greater the trajectory it gives at the expense of distance. Nos 3 and 5 are useful 'fairway woods'.

- **Irons** – These are precision clubs for mid-length shots (say 125–200 yards/ 115–180 m), and the same trajectory /distance rule applies. The irons are categorised as 'long' (nos 1–4), 'mid-' (5–7) and 'short' (8 and 9), nos 3 and 9 being the most popular.

- **Wedges** – Their large, angled heads give you the greatest loft and are good for overcoming a range of hazards – the sand wedge, for instance, to chip your way out of a bunker.

- **Putters** – The shortest of them all, designed to set the ball rolling in sprightly fashion towards the hole. (Sometimes it does.)

- **Hybrids** – Increasingly popular crosses between woods and irons.

Even a hundred years later the well-heeled golfer had only a slightly improved armoury. In 1686 Sir John Foulis of Ravelston, a dedicated sportsman who regularly played on the Leith links, records the repair of his 'play club' and the fixing of a new head on his 'lead scraper club'. It's been estimated that in those days a club may have lasted for as little as ten rounds before breaking, and buying new ones was presumably prohibitively expensive.

The range and quality of clubs steadily grew over the years, with hickory (imported to Britain from the USA) becoming the shaft wood of choice from the 1820s, but iron heads awaited the development of a stronger ball.

Although steel shafts were patented by Arthur F. Knight in 1901 (*see box right*), years passed before the golfing authorities would accept them – and when they *did* appear, the manufacturers disguised them with hickory so as not to cause too much of a shock.

A few landmark years:

- **1902**: Groove-faced irons are introduced, giving greater distance and back-spin

- **1926 (USA), 1929 (Britain)**: Steel shafts are sanctioned

- **1938 (USA), 1939 (Britain)**: The permitted number of clubs to be carried is fixed at 14

- **1952**: The Royal & Ancient and the USGA establish a unified code of rules

- **1973**: The graphite shaft is invented

## The Schenectady putter

Arthur F. Knight, from Schenectady, New York, was a keen local golfer whose otherwise skilful game faltered as soon as he reached the greens. Frustrated, he devised his own flat-headed putter with a shaft inserted in the centre, and found that it improved his game no end. Knight's odd-looking aluminium putter was greeted with some disdain at his own club, but in 1904 an early model found its way into the hands of the leading amateur golfer Walter Travis, who promptly used it to become the first American ever to win the British Amateur Championship. The rest is putting history…

# The Clubs of Yesteryear

The introduction of a numbering system for clubs in the 1930s was undoubtedly useful, but it meant doing away with some wonderful names. Here are the originals, with their rough equivalents today:

| Original | Modern equivalent |
| --- | --- |
| Brassie | No 2 wood |
| Spoon | Higher-lofted wood |
| Baffing Spoon | Approach wood |
| Cleek | No 2 iron |
| Mid mashie | 3 iron |
| Mashie Iron | 4 iron |
| Mashie | 5 iron |
| Spade mashie | 6 iron |
| Mashie niblick | 7 iron |
| Pitching niblick | 8 iron |
| Niblick | 9 iron |
| Jigger | A very low-lofted iron with a shortened shaft |

## Sabbath sticks

We've noted the Scottish kirk's disapproval of golf enthusiasts who put their sport above a preacher's sermon, and that Sunday strictness survived well into the 20th century.

If you ever attend auctions, keep an eye open for unusual walking sticks which look very much like golf clubs. This isn't an accident, because so-called 'Sabbath sticks' were designed for the enthusiast who wanted to be reminded of his passion even as he strode dutifully towards the church porch.

They date from 1890 until as late as the 1930s, with shafts of hickory, ash and other softwoods used in genuine clubs, and with heads (which fitted snugly in the palm of the golfer's hand) fashioned from persimmon and other hardwoods, as well as from brass, silver and horn.

It's not known whether, in an unobserved moment, the owners upended their canes to take in a little practice on the way home – but we'd like to think so...

# fore!

The earliest golf balls were made of wood, but for well over two hundred years (from 1618 until 1848) players were smiting a sphere made of three pieces of bull or horse hide stitched tightly around a filling of feathers.

Here's Thomas Mathieson in 1743, his poem bringing us the first ever written description of making so-called 'featheries':

*...the work of Bobson, who with matchless art*
*Shapes the firm hide, connecting every part,*
*Then in a socket sets the well-stiched void*
*And thro' the eyelet drives the downy tide;*
*Crowds urging crowds the forceful brogue impels,*
*The feathers harden and the leather swells.*

Once finished, the ball was coated with a protective white lead paint, the maker usually stamping on it both his name and its weight. And the price? Since he could make only two or three a day these balls were highly expensive, which is why players sent their 'fore-caddies' ahead of them along the course to make sure none went astray.

Calling out a warning to these golfing sniffer dogs is the probable explanation for the yell of 'fore!' which players still use today when they hit a shot into the blue yonder, desperately hoping that nobody will be maimed by it. Decent players could comfortably drive these balls a distance of some 200 yards (180m), but the Frenchman Samuel Messieux, who taught at nearby United College, is on record as having walloped a featherie all of 360 yards (330 m) at Elysian Fields, St Andrews, in 1836.

## Ginger Beer

All the holes at the St Andrews Old Course have names, and the par-4 fourth is known as Ginger Beer in honour of 'Old Da' Anderson (1821–1901), a former maker of the featherie golf balls.

When this career was over, Da became senior caddie and then keeper of the green at St Andrews before retiring and setting up a refreshment stand at the fourth hole. Here he sold the players ginger beer, milk and snacks – and apparently had a secret supply of something stronger for those in need of a 'wee nip' in the bracing Scottish weather.

# And a few other things...

Once you've bought a set of clubs and some balls you'll be pressed to buy all sorts of accessories. Do you really need them?

- **Golf shoes** – You've miles to walk, they're comfortable and they give good grip on wet grass – definitely.

- **Sun hat/visor** – The sun in your eyes is a great excuse for missing a shot, but you'll easily find some others. Get one.

- **Glove** – Only one? It's for grip, rather than to keep out the cold. A right-hander wears it on the left hand. Not essential, but a good idea.

- **Golf trolley on wheels** – Beats carrying the bag of clubs on your shoulder, so a good idea if you can afford it. If not, make sure you have a bag with double shoulder straps.

- **Golf trolley, electric** – Come on, if you're strong enough to take a swing at a golf ball you can surely pull your clubs behind you.

- **Golf cart, motorised** – If you need to drive around the course for mobility reasons, yes. Otherwise, get yourself some healthy exercise for goodness sakes!

## New balls

What do the following have in common?
 – the first transatlantic telegraph cable
 – Victorian mourning jewellery
 – pistol hand grips and rifle shoulder pads
 – moulded furniture displayed at the 1851
   Great Exhibition in Hyde Park
 – golf balls

The answer is the tropical tree gutta-percha, whose rubbery sap Western inventors suddenly 'discovered' during the 1840s and immediately put to a great variety of uses – including the insulation of that massive cable.

From our perspective it played a huge part in creating modern golf, since the technological development of powerful golf clubs needed a ball strong enough to withstand their mighty blows.

Here's a golf ball timeline:

• **1848**: Invention of the gutta-percha ball (the 'guttie'), which flies further than the featherie and is much cheaper. Its strength allows the development of iron clubs.

- **1898**: Coburn Haskell introduces a one-piece rubber core ball (the 'Bouncing Billy') in the USA. Universally adopted in 1901, it gives the average golfer an extra 20 yards (18.2 m) from the tee.

- **1905**: The first dimple-patterned golf balls are patented by William Taylor in England, maximising lift while minimising drag.

- **1990**: The American and British golf authorities agree on the size of the ball (1.68 in/4.3 cm in diameter), which becomes the standard in world golf.

Today the technological whizzkids have adopted golf in a big way – producing balls cunningly engineered to fly long and true, and fashioning lightweight, titanium alloy clubs that give the average golfer better launch angles, greater length and a larger sweet spot.

Once we've armed ourselves with all this state-of-the-art equipment we only have to knock on the door of our local golf club and begin to play.

*But will they let us in?*

# A hole in one

- The earliest recorded hole-in-one was by Old Tom Morris at the US Open in 1868.

- The youngest golfer to shoot a hole-in-one was 5-year-old Coby Orr at Littleton, Colorado, in 1975.

- The oldest was 99-year-old Otto Bucher of Switzerland at La Manga in 1985.

- Lou Kretlow notched the longest hole-in-one at the 427-yards (390m) 16th hole at Lake Hefner, Oklahoma City, in 1961.

- John Hudson, a 25-year-old professional, holed two consecutive holes-in-one, at the 11th and 12th holes, in the 1971 Martini Tournament at Norwich, England.

- In the 1973 British Open two holes-in-one were recorded at the Postage Stamp hole by the oldest and youngest competitors (Gene Sarazen and amateur David Russell).

- Mrs Argea Tissies holed in one at the 2nd hole at Punta Ala in the second round of the 1978 Italian Ladies' Senior Open. Exactly five years later, on the same date, at the same time of day, in the same round of the same tournament and at the same hole, she did it again – with the same club.

Poor Hamish had taken a wrong turn into the artisan's bar.

# CHAPTER THREE

# MEMBERS ONLY

Can you begin to imagine the sheer gut-wrenching embarrassment of it? After steadily improving your game on the municipal pay-and-play courses you've managed to persuade your local golf club that you're fit to hold one of their precious membership cards. (What, little old you?!) Now you turn up for your first 18 holes on the sacred turf – and you're sent home in disgrace. What on earth have you done? Take a look in that mirror and the terrible truth will dawn. You're wearing denim!

It's easy to mock the pretensions of the more swanky clubs, but many of them do still display the attitudes which have long made them a byword for snobbery and prejudice.

The strict dress code, which varies from club to club, is even more amusing when you consider some of the ghastly garb the professionals like to wear – loud check shirts, Argyle knitted jumpers, harlequin trousers, plus fours, tartans, baseball caps, striped shirts with plaid shorts...

But you want to know how to avoid getting banned for life, so here's a batch of well-researched tips:

- Not only no jeans, but not a trace of denim

- Shorts? Allowed at some clubs, but no gym shorts, commando trousers or cut-offs

- Caps, of course – but not back to front

- Shirts with collars, and always tucked in

- Golf shoes only: no trainers or sandals

- Socks. There's nothing that infuriates them more than bare feet inside your shoes

So much for outward appearances. You still have to know how to behave once you're out there trying to enjoy yourself. Here's our brief etiquette guide:

- Shout 'fore!' if there's a risk of hitting anyone.

- Keep behind a player who's taking a tee shot, and don't utter a word.

- Replace divots, smooth over any marks in the bunkers and repair any ball pitch and spike marks on the greens.

- Time-wasting is a crime. If you lose a ball, let the next group of players through while you look for it – and don't mark your scorecard until you're well clear of the green.

- Don't leave your bag or trolley in front of the greens.

- If you must have your mobile phone with you, switch off the ring tone.

> 'You can't call it a sport. You don't run, jump, you don't shoot, you don't pass. All you have to do is buy some clothes that don't match.'
> – Steve Sax

# A beginner's guide to golf:
## 4: Types of game

- **Stroke play** – Also known as medal play, this is a method of scoring which adds up the total number of strokes taken during a round. Most professional tournaments use this system.

- **Match play** – In match play, on the other hand, each hole is regarded individually and is worth a point. The player with the lowest number of strokes for a hole wins that point, and it's 'halved' if both players have the same score. If, say, a player is 4 holes in the lead with only 3 left to play (and therefore can't be caught), he is said to have won the match '4 and 3'.

- **Stableford** – In this system players aim to have the highest score, accumulating points hole by hole. They usually gain one point for a bogey, two for par, three for a birdie, and so on, and score nothing if they are two or more strokes over par. The idea behind the system is that players can still post a competitive total despite suffering the occasional bad hole.

## The underclass

The English are still so obsessed by class, and their elite clubs of various kinds still so strongly smack of it, that we shouldn't really be surprised to find the working man regarded as a sub-species on the golf course. Indeed, the world of golf is the only known surviving habitat of that almost extinct creature, the noble 'artisan' – as in (yes, really) 'The artisans may play on a Sunday after raking the bunkers, but they're not allowed at any time to walk in front of the clubhouse.' *And don't they dare even peep inside it!*

These lucky fellows from the world of trade have traditionally paid a relatively small amount for a decidedly inferior kind of membership – limited playing rights, separate competitions and the expectation that they help maintain the course for nothing. Many of them reinforced the class divide by breaking away from the toffs to form their own clubs, negotiating agreements to play on existing courses. Dozens still exist in today's Merry England, and they even have their own Artisan Golfers' Association.

## Blackballing

Racial discrimination in golf has usually been a surreptitious affair in England. The chief victims in years gone by were Jews who, without being officially barred from membership, found themselves mysteriously never winning quite enough votes to join. Today the laws of the land make that kind of exclusion much more difficult to get away with, but it's easy enough to hint that some people are less welcome than others.

In 2000 the Bradford businessman Jaz Athwai became the first ever Sikh golf club captain in Britain (at Waterton Park, Wakefield), but he nevertheless went on to organise the UK Asian Open Golf Society because he felt too many of his local clubs were still covertly operating a whites-only policy – officially open to all, but suddenly full when it suited them.

In melting-pot America the golf clubs (often styled country clubs) have had a wider range of 'outsiders' to exclude, among them Jews, Hispanics and African Americans.

It wasn't until 1961 – and with a great deal of reluctance – that the Professional Golfers' Association (PGA) struck the 'Caucasians-only' clause from its constitution, so allowing players of any race to take part in its tournaments. That was too late for brilliant black golfers such as Ted Rhodes and Bill Spiller, and although Charlie Sifford was able to join the circuit he was in his forties and past his best.

## A black player in the Open

John Shippen Jr, then 16 years old, was the first black player to take part in the US Open – at Shinnecock Hills, New York, in 1896.

Although these were pre-PGA days, there were predictable protests from fellow competitors because of his African origins. Shippen, however, had a Native American mother and had registered as an Indian – not quite such a terrible heritage, apparently.

He went on to play in five more US Opens, worked as a professional at several courses and made and sold his own golf clubs.

Two incidents in 1990 revealed that old habits die hard:

- Henry Bloch, co-founder of the tax preparation company H & R Block, was refused entry to the Kansas City Country Club because he was a Jew. This incensed the golfer Tom Watson, whose wife and childen were Jewish, and he promptly resigned his membership. (The club eventually relented and he rejoined.)

- During the PGA Championship at Birmingham, Alabama, the owner of the Shoal Creek club, Hall Thompson, was asked why it didn't have any black members. He replied that it simply wasn't done in Birmingham, adding in gauche self-defence, 'We don't discriminate in every other area except the blacks'. In the ensuing uproar some TV sponsors withdrew their advertising – and Thompson admitted a black member, albeit an honorary one, the very same week.

This controversy proved to be a turning point. Later that year the first black member was admitted at Augusta National – the club whose founder, Clifford Roberts, had once notoriously commented, 'As long as I'm alive golfers will be white and caddies will be black'.

Why this seismic change? It's true that Roberts *was* no longer alive (he shot himself on the banks of Augusta's little par-3 course in 1977), but what forced the club's hand was a decision taken by three of the leading administrative bodies in American golf.

## Elder statesman

Lee Elder, who in 1975 became the first African American to take part in the Masters at Augusta, travelled the country with the golf hustler 'Titanic Thompson' in his teens, earning enough playing high-stakes matches to finance a place in the PGA Tour's qualifying school.

In the weeks before his Masters appearance he received death threats from racists and had to keep moving from house to house to ensure his safety. He played a first round of 74, a second of 78 and missed the cut – but history had been made.

63

# Augusta National

- Developed in 1933 by the legendary golfer Bobby Jones and the investment dealer Clifford Roberts, the course at Augusta, Georgia has been voted the world's no. 1 time and again. It's beautiful, it's difficult to play, its greens and fairways are pampered beyond belief – and the club that owns it is just about as exclusive as they come.

- There's no point applying to join, because it doesn't work like that. You have to be invited, and the membership is limited to around 300 people. These include not only top golfers but star names in the business world such as Bill Gates and Warren Buffet.

- How much do they have to pay? No-one's saying, but the huge TV income the club receives for staging the Masters tournament every year allows fees which are little more pocket money for the kind of members it recruits. As a bonus, each is given a green jacket with the club's logo on the left breast.

- Augusta regards itself as the epitome of good etiquette and comes down hard on anyone who violates it. In 1995 the CBS commentator Gary McCord joked that the 17th green seemed to be 'bikini-waxed' because it was playing so fast. He never broadcast at the Masters again.

As a direct response to the Shoal Creek affair the PGA Tour, the PGA of America and the United States Golf Assocation stipulated that all private clubs wishing to hold tournaments must adopt membership policies 'not discriminatory against minority members or women by policy or practice'.

*Ah, women – the golf world's last frontier!*

## Up for a fight

The battle for racial equality may be almost over (helped not a little by the emergence of Tiger Woods as possibly the best golfer of all time), but golfing women know they still have a fight on their hands. They're ready for it.

Although Augusta National admitted its first black member in 1990, twenty years later it had yet to invite the first woman through the door. A previous club chairman, the wonderfully named Hootie Johnson, found himself briefly involved in a public row with the chair of the National Council of Women's Organisations (NCWO), Martha Burk. He quickly went to ground, loftily telling her in a letter that 'our membership alone decides our membership – not any outside group with its own agenda'.

When Augusta at last caves in on the issue it will be a great symbolic victory for every woman golfer who feels herself regarded as a second-class citizen in the clubhouse.

Tom was beginning to regret inviting Mary along.

So is this what you call an eagle, Tom?

In the meantime, let's raise our golfing cap to ten unquestionable stars of the women's game.

## Joyce Wethered (1901–1997)

Probably the greatest British female player of all time, she won the British Ladies Amateur Golf Championship four times (1922, 1924, 1925 and 1929) and was the English Ladies' champion for five consecutive years (1920–24). She married a baronet in 1924, becoming Lady Heathcote-Amory.

## Babe Zaharias (1911–1956)

The American Mildred 'Babe' Didrikson Zaharias (she married a wrestler known as 'The Crying Greek from Cripple Creek') was one of the most versatile athletes of all time. She excelled at a wide range of sports, entered eight qualifying events for the 1932 Olympics (winning five of them) and won the hurdles and the javelin when she got there. She broke the world record for the high jump, too, but the judges disqualified her because of her 'western roll' style.

She then moved on to golf, becoming the first American woman to win the British amateur title, before turning professional and winning 33 tournaments. In her forties she won the US Open for the third time after coming back from cancer treatment. When asked how she drove so far, she replied, 'You've got to loosen your girdle and really let the ball have it.'

> 'Golf is a game of coordination, rhythm and grace: women have these to a high degree.'
> – Babe Zaharias

## Patty Berg (1918–2006)

One of its founding members, she was a star of the Ladies Professional Golf Association (LPGA) Tour during the 1940s, 1950s and 1960s. After winning 29 amateur titles, she turned professional in 1940. She won the inagural US Women's Open in 1946 and her crop of 15 majors titles remains the all-time record by a woman golfer.

# Women's Majors

There are four 'majors' each year in the LPGA Tour, three in the United States and one in Britain – although, to complicate matters, the Ladies European Tour doesn't sanction any of the American-based tournaments. The majors are held in the same order each year:

- **Kraft Nabisco Championship** – Organised by the LPGA, this is always held at the Mission Hills Country Club in Rancho Mirage, California. By (strange) tradition the winner jumps into the pond surrounding the 18th green.

- **LPGA Championship** – An event for professionals only. The ban on amateurs was lifted in 2005 to allow the crowd- (and revenue-) drawing Michelle Wie to take part. After protests, the ban was re-imposed in 2006 – by which time Wie had turned professional.

- **US Women's Open** – Open to any amateur or professional woman golfer, without any age limits. The youngest competitor to date was 12-year-old Alexis Thompson in 2007.

- **Women's British Open** – Established in 1976 by the Ladies' Golf Union as the equivalent of the men's British Open.

## Louise Suggs (b. 1923)

They called her 'Little Miss Poker Face' because of the grimly determined manner in which she concentrated on each hole. 'The single greatest lesson to be learned from golf,' she once said, 'is mental discipline.' The seriousness worked: she won 55 professional tournaments, including 11 majors, and was US women's champion twice.

## Betsy Rawls (b. 1928)

Elizabeth 'Betsy' Rawls obviously learned fast. She didn't pick up a golf club until she was 17, but she finished runner-up to Babe Zaharias in the US Women's Open in 1950 and then, having turned professional, won the tournament the following year – the first of her record four Open victories.

'I have always had a drive that pushed me to try for perfection,' she once said, 'and golf is a game in which perfection stays just out of reach.' But only just.

# A beginner's guide to golf:
## 5. Handicapping

The handicapping system is horribly complicated, but here's a brief outline to get you started.

- It isn't used in the professional game.

- Its intention is to allow players of different abilities to compete on equal terms.

- Amateur players have personal handicaps which vary according to their performances over time. (A zero handicap would make you a 'scratch' golfer.)

- If the par for a course – the number of strokes a scratch player should take to go round it – is 72 and your likely total is 90 you have a handicap of 18 – which isn't bad at all.

- Imagine that you're playing a friend who has a 9 handicap. He's obviously better than you, but if he goes round the course in his expected 81 strokes (72 plus 9) while you manage 89, you've won.

Why? Take that 9 handicap from his round of 81 and that leaves 72. Now take your 18 handicap from 89 – your 71 is the lower, and therefore the winning, score. Simple!

## Mickey Wright (b. 1935)

Was Mary 'Mickey' Wright the eighth best player of all time (men included), as *Golf Magazine* decided in 2009, or only the ninth, as *Golf Digest* suggested a year later? No matter: both ranked her as the greatest ever woman golfer, while the great Ben Hogan reckoned her swing was the best he'd seen. Wright won 12 majors between 1958 and 1966 and is the only player in LPGA Tour history to have held all four major titles at the same time.

## Jo-Anne Carner (b. 1939)

Known affectionately as 'Big Mama', she is the only woman to have won the U.S. Girls' Junior, U.S. Women's Amateur and U.S. Women's Open titles, and the first person ever to win three different USGA championship events.

In 2004 she became the oldest player to make a cut on the LPGA Tour – at the age of 65.

# Kathy Whitworth (b. 1939)

Throughout her career the Texan won 88 LPGA Tour tournaments, more than anyone else has won on either the LPGA Tour or the PGA Tour, and in 1981 she became the first woman to reach career earnings of $1 million.

As a young woman she had been overweight, but it was as a lean and fit competitor that she won her many titles. 'I'd probably be the fat lady in the circus if it hadn't been for golf,' Whitworth said. 'It kept me out of the refrigerator.'

# Nancy Lopez (b. 1957)

This lively Mexican-American burst onto the professional scene in 1978, winning five tournaments in a row during her first full season on the LPGA Tour, and nine in all. For good measure she also won the Vare Trophy for lowest scoring average, was voted LPGA Rookie of the Year and Player of the Year and was named Associated Press Female Athlete of the Year. Oh, and she also appeared on the cover of *Sports Illustrated*.

Career breaks to have her three daughters probably played a part in her failing to win the US Women's Open, although she came second no fewer than four times.

In retirement she developed her company, Nancy Lopez Golf, which makes a range of women's clubs and accessories.

## Laura Davies (b. 1963)

The modern world of golf is dominated by Americans, which makes Laura Davies' achievement all the more remarkable. The most accomplished English woman golfer of her generation, winning the Ladies European Tour (LET) Order of Merit a record seven times between 1985 and 2006, she's also the first non-American to have finished at the top of the LPGA money list.

Davies is keen on other sports, too. At the 1996 Evian Masters in France she was fined by the LET for watching an England versus Spain European Championship football match on a portable television during the final round. She went on to win it.

# What happened to Michelle?

In 2006 a *Time* magazine article named the 17-year-old golf prodigy Michelle Wie 'one of a hundred people who shape our world'.

All sports need glamour, and Wie promised to provide it. She'd turned professional shortly before her sixteenth birthday, signing multi-million dollar sponsorship deals with Nike and Sony, and the crowds flocked to watch her.

And then she stopped winning. As flop followed flop the media focused on her every slip – the golfer as fallen celebrity. How would those stars of yesteryear have coped?

> 'A passion, an obsession, a romance, a nice acquaintanceship with trees, sand and water.'
> – Bob Ryan

**H**arry hoped to do a bit of subtle wheeling and dealing during the match.

# CHAPTER FOUR

# PLEASED TO MEET YOU!

# G

olf obsessives who worry endlessly about the state of their swing and the smoothness of their putting may believe that nothing but their talent (or otherwise) is on show as they fret from hole to hole. If only! Four hours shared company on a golf course equates to a bruising session on a Freudian couch. Character traits usefully disguised in the bustle of an office or a bar are cruelly exposed as you tramp the long fairways with all your personal habits on view and only your own voice to break the silence.

# A beginner's guide to golf: 6. Types of team games

- **Foursomes** – A sociable form of golf for two teams of two. Each team has a single ball, which the pair take it in turn to play. They also alternate the teeing off at each hole.

- **Four ball** – The same team set-up as foursomes, but each player has his own ball and the one taking the fewest shots for a hole wins it for his team. Because each team has two opportunities, the players can afford to be take more risks.

- **Ambrose** – For teams of two or four. Each player hits his own ball, and the position of the team's best shot is selected as the starting point for the next round of strokes by all its members – and so on. Kind to less skilful players.

- **Greensomes** – For two teams of two. The Ambrose system is used for the tee shots, but thereafter the players take alternate shots in the usual way.

Although romances have been known to blossom on the greens it's much more likely that prolonged subjection to a companion's irritating prattle and repulsive physical tics will pour buckets of water over any flickering flames of love.

## Pitching for a job

Businessmen don't have much of a reputation for psychological subtlety, but they've long worked on the assumption that the golf course is somewhere you can't hide.

Some organise staff tournaments, looking out for what it tells them about their workers – whether they're 'team players', can handle pressure and resist the urge to cheat. Others will in effect interview senior employees by taking them round the course and judging whether they're fit for promotion.

In 2010 a UK company went so far as to build a small indoor golf course at its European HQ in order to test potential top-level recruits when they came for a job interview. Its managing director explained that 'nothing shows a candidate's true colours better than getting competitive. A can-do personality is the only thing that will ensure our team provides outstanding service to our customers.' This is what he was trying to find out:

- **Courage**: do candidates opt for big shots (a hole-in-one approach) or lots of shorter shots?

- **Multi-tasking**: can the candidate think, speak and play at once?

- **Winning mentality**: does the potential recruit compete hard, or are they careful to let the interviewer win?

- **Bouncing back**: how does the interviewee cope with a miss? What is their response?

- **Strategy & planning**: how effective is the candidate's game plan and shot play?

- **Adaptability**: how do candidates deal with increasing levels of complexity and difficulty around the course?

That's looking at it from the employer's point of view. But what if you're the poor mutt who's dragged onto the golf course in the knowledge that your present or future job is on the line?

The important thing to realise is that the standard of your golf isn't an issue. If your tormentor is mad keen on the sport you obviously shouldn't deride it, but he can't expect you to play beyond your capabilities. Just examine those bullet points on the facing page – and decide whether you really want to put yourself through all this after all.

## Jaw~jaw

Winston Churchill (who compared golf to 'chasing a quinine pill around a cow pasture'), famously said that jaw-jaw (talking) was preferable to war-war. He was only an occasional player of the game himself, but many politicans and businessmen have been drawn to golf, not least because of the opportunity it gives them to jaw-jaw and strike deals well away from the eyes of the prying world.

> '**Eighteen holes of match or medal play will teach you more about your foe than will 18 years of dealing with him across a desk.**'
> **– Grantland Rice**

# Political golfers

The boom in British golf at the turn of the 19th and 20th centuries has been largely attributed to Arthur Balfour, prime minister from 1902–1905 and (as foreign secretary) later the author of the Balfour Declaration which supported a Jewish homeland in Palestine.

A Scot, Balfour served as captain of both the Royal & Ancient at St Andrews and the North Berwick golf club. He played so often and so enthusiastically – if not particularly well – that the satirical magazine Punch dubbed him 'The Golfour'.

The golf-mad war hero **General Dwight D. Eisenhower** ('Ike') didn't let becoming president of the United States get in the way of his sport. During the eight years of his presidency (1953–61) he fitted in no fewer than 800 rounds of golf, and he had a putting green installed on the White House lawn.

He's well remembered at Augusta National, where there's Ike's Pond (he suggested where they might site it), Eisenhower Cabin (built for him by the members when he was elected president, sports an eagle over the porch) and Eisenhower Tree (a loblolly pine which he hit so many times when teeing off that he suggested it be cut down).

Most American presidents of modern times have been golfers, though few have been much good at it:

- **John F. Kennedy** was an exception, but he'd criticised Eisenhower for playing so much golf as president and therefore had to sneak out of the White House to play in secret.

- Some of the others weren't above a little cheating. When Sam Snead played against **Richard Nixon** the president seemed to have lost his ball in a thicket, but it suddenly flew out of the woods onto the fairway. 'I knew he threw it out,' Snead said, 'but I didn't say anything.' (Of course not.)

- **Bill Clinton** made up for his poor play by asking for a succession of mulligans and gimmes (*see page 85*), while **Gerald Ford** was so innacurate that he contrived to hit several spectators during his golfing 'career'.

- The comedian Bob Hope produced a constant flow of Ford jokes. 'Whenever I play with him,' he said, 'I usually try to make it a foursome – the president, myself, a paramedic and a faith healer.'

> **'Golf always makes me so damned angry.'**
> **– King George V**

83

A survey of business executives by a leading US hotels group found that the golf course remains an important trading post:

- **93 per cent** agreed that golfing with a business associate was a good way to establish a closer relationship.

- **80 per cent** said they found golfing a good way to make new business contacts.

- **35 per cent** reported that some of their biggest business deals were made on the golf course.

## Best behaviour

We've already covered some of the basic etiquette, but what are the unwritten rules for spending half a day out on the links in the hope of brokering a deal? This is the time to introduce you to some quaint golfing terms.

- **Sandbagging** – Before you begin your match you'll need to agree on the handicaps you're both playing under. Honesty is the only policy here. Sandbagging is giving yourself a higher handicap than is justified – in other words, saying you're a worse player than you really are so that you've a greater chance of winning. It's a ploy used by the unscrupulous when money is involved, and it will give you serious embarrassment if you're found out. You don't need to win, remember – it's the contract you're after.

- **Mulligan** – More often used in the US than Britain, and sometimes known as a 'do-over', this is simply an agreement to overlook a terrible shot, especially when teeing off, and taking another one. (It is, needless to say, quite outside the rules of golf.) Make sure you agree this with your companion first or a lot of bad feeling will ensue.

  Nobody knows how the name arose. Since a second shot even worse than the first is known as a **Finnegan**, the suspicion has to be that it's a little joke at the expense of Irish-Americans.

- **Gimme** (as in 'give it to me') – This is a putt which other players can agree as having been sunk without the shot having actually been played. The assumption is that it was so easy that it couldn't be missed anyway. A gimme isn't allowed under stroke play rules, but you'll see professionals offer them in match play. If your business deal partner requests a gimme you'll of course agree, but unless you know him well it's probably best not to ask the favour yourself.

Finally a few pieces of sage advice from those who've been there and done it:

- Make sure not to humiliate or condescend to your opponent, however awful his golf may be. The amount of time you actually spend hitting the ball is minuscule: concentrate on building up the business relationship instead.

- If you're the competitive type who usually likes to bet a round of drinks to give the match a bit of needle, forget it! It's not that your companion can't afford to buy you a gin and tonic in the clubhouse bar, but he won't be impressed if you seem to play as if it matters.

- Don't discuss business before the 5th hole or after the 15th – the pretence is that you're merely enjoying the game.

- Don't expect to tie up the deal as soon as you reach the clubhouse. Give him room to breathe and sooner or later he'll be back in touch. *Success!*

# More golf quotations

'Golf is a good walk spoiled.'

Mark Twain

'If a lot of people gripped a knife and fork the way they do a golf club, they'd starve to death.'

Sam Snead

'Golf is an ineffectual attempt to put an elusive ball into an obscure hole with implements ill-adapted to the purpose.'

President Woodrow Wilson

'Golf seems to me an arduous way to go for a walk. I prefer to take the dogs out.'

Princess Anne

'All I've got against it is that it takes you so far away from the clubhouse.'

Erik Linklater

# A beginner's guide to golf: 7. The shots you make

*(assuming a right-handed player)*

- **Air shot** – Also known as a **whiff**, this is an attempt to strike the ball which fails completely. Sorry, but you lose a stroke for this.

- **Approach shot** – One intended to land on the green.

- **Blast** – A bunker shot that sends the ball onto the green. Also known as an **explosion**.

- **Block** – Otherwise a **push**, a shot played severely to the right.

- **Bump and run** – A low-trajectory shot intended to set the ball rolling along the fairway onto the green.

- **Chip** – A short shot that travels through the air over a short distance and rolls towards the hole.

- **Cut** – A shot which curves from left to right.

- **Draw** – A shot that curves to the left. If overdone it becomes a **hook**.

- **Duck-hook** – An extremely low hook, barely airborne.

- **Fade** – A shot that curves slightly to the right.

- **Flop shot** – A short shot designed to travel very high in the air and land softly on the green.

- **Hook** – A poor shot curving sharply to the left.

- **Knock-down** – A low-trajectory shot, usually to combat a strong wind.

- **Pull** – A poor shot which goes directly left, rather than curving like a hook.

- **Punch shot** – A low-trajectory shot to avoid trees.

- **Push** – A shot played severely to the right.

- **Shank** – A ghastly shot off the wrong part of the club.

- **Slice** – A poor shot which curves sharply to the right.

- **Shrimp** – A hook so severe that it resembles the shape of a shrimp.

- **Thin shot** – A poor shot, with the clubhead striking too high on the ball.

- **Topped shot** – Oops! The clubhead strikes the top of the ball so that it merely rolls or bounces.

- **Tree shot** – You've guessed it: so bad a shot that it hits leaves and branches, with the ball ending up way short of its target.

Vijay Singh

Sam Snead

Ben Hogan

Phil Mickelson

Ernie Els

Harry Vardon

# CHAPTER FIVE

# GOLFING GREATS

I n a sport regarded almost as a religion by its adherents, the stars who emerge generation by generation to enthrall us with their uncanny skill take on the stature of saints, their election to the 'golf hall of fame' a kind of beatification.

We've already paid tribute to some of the leading women players. In this chapter we do the same for thirty male golfing giants who have graced the game since the middle of the 19th century. They're presented in chronological order to prevent any argument about their ranking – but we still expect some grumbles about those left out.

# World Golf Hall of fame

Twenty-six organisations all over the world support the hall of fame which, in a single site at St Augustine, Florida, represents both men and women. Its museum features exhibits on the game's history, heritage and techniques; its major players and organisations; golf course design, equipment and dress; and new developments in the game.

Members are inducted on a points system in one of five categories: PGA Tour/Champions Tour, LPGA Tour, Lifetime Achievement, International and Veterans.

The first eleven men inducted, in 1975, included nine Americans, one Englishman (Harry Vardon) and a South African (Gary Player). The women had already had their own hall of fame, and six were drafted into the new combined system in 1975 – all of them American.

Apart from the world's top players, the list includes famous 'celebrity friends' of golf such as **Bing Crosby**, **Bob Hope**, **Dinah Shore** and **Dwight D. Eisenhower**, and individuals who have given the game service in a variety of ways, as administrators, golf course architects, writers, promoters, agents and so on.

# Old Tom Morris (1821-1908)

Born at St Andrews, the 'home of golf', this weaver's son took up the sport in the most rudimentary way at the age of ten, using a home-made club to hit wine bottle corks pierced with nails (the nearest things to balls he could find) around the local streets.

By the time he was 14 he had progressed from caddying to serve as an apprentice to Allan Robertson, widely regarded as the first ever professional golfer and the best in the world at that time. He lost his job when Robertson, who manufactured featherie golf balls, caught him practising with one of the new gutties. Sheer treachery!

Morris now moved to Prestwick, where he laid out the new course and ran his own golf equipment business, though he later moved back to St Andrews to improve the Old Course there for the Royal & Ancient.

He was a main mover in the inauguration of the Open championship in 1860 (he struck the very first shot and came second), and went on to win it four times. He still holds the record for being the oldest ever Open champion – at the age of 46.

Morris introduced new features in course design and is regarded as the father of modern greens-keeping. At the age of 86 he fell down a flight of stairs at the New Golf Club in St Andrews, cracked his skull and died. His grave in the grounds of St Andrews Cathedral is a mecca for golfers the world over.

## Young Tom Morris (1851–1875)

His life began with great promise and ended in tragedy. As Old Tom's son he was bound to have golf in his blood, and he soon proved himself to be an even better player, winning four Open championships by the age of 21. (His first triumph, at the age of 17, ensures him a place in the records books as the youngest majors champion in golf history.)

In 1875, partnering his father in a team match against the brothers Willie and Mungo Park, he received a telegram urging his immediate return home, where his wife Margaret was experiencing a difficult pregnancy. By the time he arrived, both his wife and the newborn baby were dead. Young Tom followed them less than four months later – a classic case of dying of a broken heart.

## Harry Vardon (1870–1937)

Born in Jersey in the Channel Islands, Vardon began playing sport in his teens and was so good that he'd turned professional by the age of twenty. He went on to win six British Opens (still a record) and one US Open in a total of 62 tournament victories – 14 of them (another record) in a row.

*Trivia note*: Vardon was the first golfer to wear the baggy, but comfortable, knickerbockers.

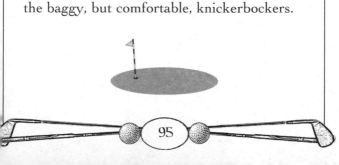

# A beginner's guide to golf:
## 8. Getting a grip

There are three basic grips in common use today, and you'll need to practise endlessly to decide which is best for you.

- For the **Vardon grip**, first popularised by Harry Vardon, a right-handed player puts the little finger of the right hand over the index finger of the left hand.

- In the **interlocking grip**, used by many leading players, the little fingers of both hands are locked together.

- The **baseball grip** has the hands together without any overlap.

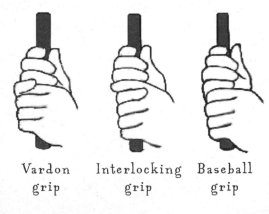

Vardon      Interlocking      Baseball
grip            grip              grip

# Walter Hagen (1892–1969)

The Americans had arrived, and Hagen wafted a breath of bracing air into the stuffy world of British golf. A consummate player (he won the British Open four times, the US Open twice and 11 majors in all), he was also an assertive character who took nonsense from no-one and who literally added colour to the course with his bright clothing, plus-fours and two-toned shoes.

'I never wanted to be a millionaire,' he once said, 'just to live like one' – but his many lucrative exhibition matches and product endorsements made him the first sporting millionaire in any case. As for living like one, he spent his fortune conspicuously and travelled with suitcases stuffed with cash.

# Bobby Jones (1902–1971)

Unlike his fellow American Walter Hagen, Jones remained an amateur all his playing life. A darling of the crowds, he was the only sportsman to be given two ticker-tape parades in New York City.

Having taken degrees in both mechanical engineering and English literature, he passed his bar exams in a year and became an attorney. He retired from the game at the age of 28, having (uniquely) achieved the then Grand Slam of the Open and Amateur championships in both the US and Britain within a single calendar year.

His sporstmanship was exemplified in the 1925 US Open when, about to play out of the rough, he accidentally moved the ball a fraction. He immediately gave himself the stipulated two-stroke penalty, although none of the marshals had been aware of it – and then lost the tournament by a single stroke. A noble gesture? Jones would have none of it: 'You may as well praise a man for not robbing a bank,' he said.

After his retirement he remained involved with the sport, and turned professional to make instructional golf films. He co-designed the Augusta National course with Alister MacKenzie and founded the Masters Tournament in 1934.

# Enter the pros

The well-heeled English have always loved the amateur ideal in their sports, and that often meant treating the lesser beings who earned a living from them with an unpleasant haughtiness.

Then, as now, the golf club pro was an invaluable figure (repairing clubs, giving lessons and advice, looking after the shop and so on) but he wasn't allowed to enter the clubhouse by the front door or, in many cases, make use of its facilities. He was the equivalent of 'trade', and was expected to know his place.

Visiting professional golfers were treated in much the same way. In 1920, when refused entry to the club's dressing room at the British Open in Deal, Kent, Walter Hagen ostentatiously hired a Rolls-Royce limousine to change in.

Some of the clubs back home were infected by British snobbery, too. At the US Open that same year Hagen organised a collection among the players to present a grandfather clock to the host club – thanking them for allowing the professionals to use their clubhouse.

All pros, Gene Sarazen later acknowledged, 'should say a silent thanks to Walter Hagen each time they stretch a cheque between their fingers'.

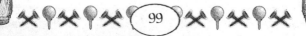

## Gene Sarazen (1902-1999)

Born Eugenio Saraceni in New York, this son of an Italian carpenter changed his name to Sarazen because he thought it sounded better on the golf course. Apart from his many tournament victories, he's remembered as the man who invented the sand wedge (*see page 43*), winning the 1932 British Open with it after managing to keep it secret during the preliminary rounds. Sarazen said he came up with the revolutionary design after studying aircraft movement when taking flying lessons from his friend, the eccentric millionaire Howard Hughes.

With his new wedge he developed the technique, now commonly used, of contacting the sand a couple of inches behind the ball ('exploding' it) rather than hitting the ball itself. Today's top golfers also began to use the sand wedge on grass, leading to a revolution in 'short game' techniques.

Sarazen's most glorious on-course moment came in 1935 with 'the shot heard around the world' (*see page 37*). He needed to win the

Masters in order to complete the Grand Slam
of all four major titles, but as he approached
the 5-par 15th hole he was all of three strokes
behind the leader, Craig Wood, who had
already finished his round – and whose name
had already been written on the winner's
cheque.

Sarazen's second shot carried all of 235 yards
straight into the hole, so cancelling Wood's
advantage in a single stroke. He went on to
win the play-off the next day.

## Jimmy Demaret (1910–1983)

The American professional was the first three-
time winner of the Masters. Known for his
colourful dress sense and a keen sense of
humour, Demaret later became a golf
commentator, co-hosted Shell's 'Wonderful
World of Golf' with Gene Sarazen and was a
guest on the 'I Love Lucy' show in the 1950s.
He died while getting ready for another round
of golf.

# Ben Hogan (1912-1997)

Most professionals agree that Ben Hogan was the best striker of a golf ball ever, with a swing perfected over hours and hours of practice. His early success was greeted with respect rather than adulation, however, as he was an introverted character who fixed his opponents with a steely glare and rarely spoke.

The crowds only warmed to him after a terrible car smash in 1949, which left him with multiple fractures and the threat of never walking again. In fact 'The Hawk' was back playing golf within the year, and a few months later won his second US Open.

In 1951, limping and unable to complete more than 18 holes in a day, he won the Masters, the US Open and the World Championship of Golf, and finished second and fourth in the only other two tournaments he entered. In 1953 he added the British Open to his tally, so equalling Gene Sarazen's Grand Slam.

Hogan's life was celebrated in the film 'Follow the Sun', starring Glenn Ford.

## Sam Snead (1912–2002)

Although undoubtedly one of the greats, winning seven majors, he never managed to win the US Open, taking second place no fewer than four times. Like Hogan, he had a brilliant swing, which won him the nickname 'Slammin' Sammy', but he's also known for a hillbilly pose which saw him competing in bare feet and wearing a straw hat.

## Byron Nelson (1912–2006)

In 1945 Nelson won 18 of the 35 PGA tournaments, including 11 in a row – both records which are yet to be beaten. He promptly retired to become a rancher, although he returned to the fold as a golf commentator and was the first professional ever to have a PGA tour event named after him.

> 'Golf is played by twenty million mature American men whose wives think they are out having fun.'
> – Jim Bishop

## Bobby Locke (1917-1987)

The first internationally successful South African golfer, Locke entered his first British Open in 1936, when he was only 18, and turned professional two years later. His career was interrupted by the second world war (he served in his country's air force), but he resumed it in style: invited by Sam Snead, he joined the PGA's American tour in 1947, and won six tournaments – four in just five weeks.

## The golfers who riled Hitler

As if watching Jesse Owens take four golds at the 1936 Berlin Olympics wasn't bad enough, the Führer also had his nose put out of joint by a couple of golfers from northern England.

An amateur international tournament had been arranged at Baden-Baden immediately after the Games, with a brass salver donated by Hitler. A German pair seemed assured of victory in the foursomes – only for Tommy Thirsk and Arnold Bentley to stage a magnificent comeback. The story goes that Hitler set out to present the salver himself, but turned back home when he heard the result.

His strongest point was his finishing on the green. 'You drive for show, but putt for dough,' he said. But he seemed to annoy Americans by taking home so much of their prize money. He was banned in 1949, allegedly over a dispute about playing commitments, and although the ban was lifted two years later he preferred to play in Africa and Europe – winning the British Open four times in all.

## Arnold Palmer (b. 1929)

The bright star of golf's television age – handsome, with a dashing style and wearing his heart on his sleeve – he was urged on to his many tournament victories by a group of loyal and vociferous supporters known as 'Arnie's Army'.

He was the first golfer signed up by the sports agent Mark McCormack, and he made a fortune from his business activities (including course design) as well as his golf.

*Trivia note*: An 'Arnold Palmer' is a beverage comprising half iced tea and half lemonade.

## Peter Thomson (b. 1929)

The Australian won five British Opens (he was the only player in the 20th century to win three in a row) and claimed the national championships of no fewer than ten countries overall.

Thomson was also a writer on golf, filing articles for the *Melbourne Age* for some 50 years, and he designed several courses in his native country.

## Gary Player (b. 1935)

Known variously as 'Mr Fitness', 'the Black Knight' and 'the International Ambassador of Golf', the South African recorded 165 tournament wins worldwide over six decades, a tally which included nine Majors.

Another player who turned golf course architect (designing more than 300 throughout the world), Player has a far wider range of interests than most, including property development, publishing and a stud farm breeding thoroughbred race horses. He also runs The Player Foundation, which promotes education for the underprivileged around the world.

*Trivia note*: Player is estimated to have notched up 15 million travelling miles during his golfing career.

## Bob Charles (b. 1936)

Sir Bob Charles (a New Zealander knighted in 1999) became the first left-handed player to win a Major when he took the British Open title in 1963, and he's the only 'lefty' in golf's hall of fame.

Having won some 80 tournaments all over the globe he joined the Senior PGA Tour and at 71 twice 'beat his age' – went round in less than 71, that is – in a single tournament. In 2010, now 74 years old, he announced that it was at last time to pack his golf bag and retire.

'I've been travelling this world for 50 years,' he explained, 'and it's time to slow down and spend more time on my farm in New Zealand with my family.'

## Jack Nicklaus (b. 1940)

The 'Golden Bear' (he was big, blonde and beefy) features in every list of the world's top ten golfers. He entered the professional fray in 1961 and was immediately pitched into a head-to-head confrontation with the crowd's favourite, his fellow American Arnold Palmer.

Nicklaus went on to become the first player to complete first the double and then the triple 'slam' of all four professional major championships. When he won the 18th and last of them at the 1986 Masters he was Augusta's oldest ever winner, at 46.

Yet another course designer (his company is one of the biggest in the world), he has also written several books, the most influential being *Golf My Way*.

> 'Playing the game I have learned the meaning of humility. It has given me an understanding of the futility of human effort.'
> – Abba Eban

# Ray Floyd (b. 1942)

Had the American won the Masters in 1990 (he came agonisingly close, losing to Nick Faldo in the play-off), he would have achieved the remarkable feat of having won major championships in four different decades. His first had been the PGA in 1969, followed by the Masters in 1976, the PGA again in 1982 and the US Open in 1986.

Floyd's speciality was the chip shot from the longer grass just off the green. One of the most audacious came in the 1980 Doral-Eastern Open, in a sudden-death play-off with Jack Nicklaus. On the second hole he chipped the ball in for a birdie – and won the title.

# Tony Jacklin (b. 1944)

His most glorious moment as a player was on June 21st, 1970, when he sank a putt to become the first Briton in 49 years to win the US Open. This beat his achievement the previous year of being the first in 18 years to win the British Open.

Those were Jacklin's only two victories in major championships, but he later went on to become the most successful European captain in Ryder Cup history.

## Tom Watson (b. 1949)

An exceptional bad weather player, the American was well suited to the blustery links – and he accordingly won the British Open no fewer than five times, as against a single win in the US Open and two in the Masters.

### The greatest shot ever?

The cable network company ESPN named Tom Watson's chip at the 17th hole in the 1982 US Open as 'the greatest shot in golf history'.

Watson (tied with Jack Nicklaus, who had already finished his round), found himself in the rough with a difficult stroke to make towards a fast and sloping green.

His chip shot flew unerringly towards the hole, hit the flag stick and dropped in for a birdie. He followed it with another birdie at the 18th – and won the coveted title for the only time.

The world no. 1 from 1978 until 1982, he had an intense, though friendly, rivalry with Jack Nicklaus. He also had staying power. At the age of 59, sixteen years after winning the last of his five Open titles, he led the tournament going into the final round (the oldest man ever to have done so) only to lose in the play-off.

## Ben Crenshaw (b. 1952)

Few golfers win the very first professional tournament they enter, but the Texan did. He later won two Masters eleven years apart and served as the US Ryder Cup captain.

Putting was Crenshaw's speciality, and he learned his remarkable skills from the coach Harvey Penick. His second Masters victory, in 1995, came a week after Penick's death. Crenshaw, emotionally charged, putted to perfection, never needing more than two shots on any green in any round of the tournament.

And his philosophy? 'If we are to preserve the integrity of golf as left to use by our forefathers,' he said, 'it is up to all of us to carry on the true spirit of the game.'

## Greg Norman (b. 1955)

Blond, aggressive and Australian, he was known as 'The Great White Shark' but closing in for the kill often proved beyond him. Although Norman spent 331 weeks as the world's no. 1 ranked golfer during his career, won the British Open twice and was one of the greatest money earners of his day, he habitually drew close to winning the big events only to throw the chance away.

His worst experience was at the US Open in 1996. He began the final round with a lead of six strokes but contrived to lose the match to Nick Faldo by five: Faldo went round in 67, whereas Norman's score was a sorry 78.

## Bernhard Langer (b. 1957)

Germany's only representative in our Top 30 won the Masters twice, and was the very first world no. 1 when the rankings began in 1986. Through much of his career, however, Langer's short game suffered from an endless battle with the 'yips' (*see facing page*) – prompting him to change his grip many times.

# A beginner's guide to golf: 9. Some useful terms

- **Address** – The act of setting yourself up for a shot, with the clubhead behind the ball.

- **Away** – The player furthest from the hole – who should always play first.

- **Divot** – A chunk of grass dislodged when your club hits the turf. Replace it or fill the hole with sand.

- **Flagstick** – Otherwise, the pin. It shows you where the hole is.

- **Grounding** – Placing the clubface on the ground behind the ball – not allowed when playing from a bunker or other hazard.

- **Lie** – How the ball rests on the ground. Good or bad.

- **Loose impediments** – Small stones, leaves etc. You can remove them, but you mustn't move the ball.

- **Play through** – Permission granted by slow players to allow a speedier group to overtake them.

- **Unplayable** – What you can designate your ball in an impossible position. There are strict rules about where you can relocate it – and you drop a stroke.

- **The Yips** – A tendency to twitch during putting.

## Seve Ballesteros (b. 1957)

In contrast with Langer, the Spanish former world no. 1 was known for his erratic driving but nerveless play on the greens. He burst onto the golfing scene at the age of 19 by finishing runner-up in the British Open, and he won five major tournaments between 1979 and 1988 – his 1980 Masters victory being the first by a European.

His brilliance extended to match play, and he won the world championship in that discipline no fewer than five times. In the Ryder Cup he created a formidable partnership with his fellow Spaniard José Maria Olazábal, the pair winning 11 of their 15 matches, with two halved.

In 2008 Ballesteros was admitted to hospital with a brain tumour. The following year, after lengthy operations and chemotherapy, he announced the founding of the Seve Ballesteros Foundation. He said it would help cancer research, especially in the field of brain tumours, but would also help young golfers in financial difficulties.

# Nick Faldo (b. 1957)

The Englishman borrowed a friend's club after watching Jack Nicklaus in the 1971 Masters. Within four years he had won the English Amateur and the British Youths Championship. He then turned professional.

He was called 'Nick Foldo' in the British press after his game collapsed in the 1983 Open and the 1984 Masters, but he remodelled his troublesome swing and by the late 1980s had become the best player on the circuit: between 1987 and 1996 he won more of the majors (six) than any other player, and was known for his nerveless demeanour.

Faldo was the most successful player in the history of the Ryder Cup (and later became Europe's captain), but from 2004 his tournament appearances dwindled as he developed a new career in golf broadcasting.

## Ian Woosnam (b. 1958)

Born in the same era as a clutch of first-class golfers, the Welshman had to settle for the Masters as his only major title, but in the year he won it (1991) he also rose to the top in the world rankings. He was also the first player to win the World Match Play Championship in three different decades.

*Trivia note*: Woosnam was one of the smallest professional golfers at 5 ft 4½ inches (1.538 m).

## A golfer's farewell

The colourful American player Payne Stewart was killed in an air crash in 1999, eight months after winning the US Open.

At the following Open a dinner was given in his honour, and the next morning the players and fans mustered by the 18th fairway to pay him a fitting tribute.

Twenty of the players and Payne's long-time caddie Mike Hicks simultaneously drove golf balls into the water – golf's equivalent of a 21-gun salute.

## Sandy Lyle (b. 1958)

The Scot's two major titles were the Open at Sandwich in 1985 and the Masters in 1988. The first Briton ever to win at Augusta, he was tied with Mark Calcavecchia at the 18th and drove his tee-shot into a bunker. Under enormous pressure he then hit a sublime seven iron which rolled to within twelve feet of the hole. He sunk the putt and won.

That same year Lyle won the World Match Play Championship, having previously been a losing finalist several times.

## Vijay Singh (b. 1963)

'The Big Fijian' (not the most imaginative of nicknames) was known for his meticulous approach to the game, spending hours on the course before and after matches to analyse his game.

He spent 32 weeks as the top-ranked player in the world during 2004–5, and won three majors – the Masters in 2000 and the PGA Championship in 1998 and 2004.

## Ernie Els (b. 1969)

The South African, known as 'The Big Easy' because of his size and relaxed style, won the US Open in 1994 and 1997 and the British Open in 2002. He was also a runner-up in major tournaments six times, too. In 1996 he also became the third player to win the World Match Play Championship three times in a row, and he added a fourth title six years later.

## Grounds for divorce

The Scottish golfer Colin Montgomerie doesn't make our top 30 because, despite his many other triumphs, he never won one of the majors.

On the course he had the reputation of being a bit of a grump, throwing temper tantrums and demanding that the crowd, TV crews or officials move away or be quiet while he played.

Did he care a bit too much? His first wife clearly thought so. When she divorced him she cited 'unreasonable behaviour due to his obsession with golf'.

## Phil Mickelson (b. 1970)

So often the nearly man, Mickelson six times came second or third in major tournaments between 1999 and 2003 before he at last turned the corner. Then he won three in three years (the Masters twice, sandwiching the PGA Championship) and notched another Masters in 2010.

A natural right-hander, Mickelson adopted a left-handed swing (earning him the nickname 'Lefty'), apparently because as a lad he watched his father's right-hand swing and mirrored it.

*Trivia note*: After his wayward tee shot broke a spectator's watch during the 2006 Ford Championship at Doral, Mickelson gave the man $200 in compensation.

## Tiger Woods (b. 1975)

By 2009 the self-styled 'Cablinasian' – Caucasian, Black, (American) Indian and Asian – was estimated to have earned more than a billion dollars from winnings and endorsements since turning professional in 1996, making him the richest athlete in the world. By that time he had already won 14 major championships (second only to Jack Nicklaus's 18), had become the youngest player to achieve a career grand slam and had achieved more major wins and PGA Tour wins than any player of his generation.

And then his life imploded. He confessed that he had failed to live up to the Buddhist ideals of restraint he'd been brought up with, and in 2010 he paid the penalty with a divorce from his Swedish wife Elin. After a short break from the game he returned to the circuit, but in those first few months his old flair was nowhere to be seen.

*Was this a permanent decline? Golf needs its heroes, and many an aficionado was hoping that their fallen star would soon be shooting through the firmament again.*

Well, I do like a birdie or two!

Tiger hoped to lift his life out of the rough as quickly as possible.

# The four majors

There are four major championships each year, three in the United States and one in Britain, always staged in the same chronological order. Winning all four at different times give a player a 'career slam'; winning all the majors in the same calendar year (never yet achieved) would be the 'grand slam'.

**The Masters, April** – Played at Augusta since its inception in 1934, it's the only major which never changes its venue.
- A legendary golfer always hits an honorary tee-shot on the morning of the first round.
- A green jacket is awarded to the winner, but it must be returned to the clubhouse after a year.
- Jack Nicklaus has won more Masters than any other golfer.

**The US Open, June** – Simply known as the Open in the States, it's hosted by the United States Golf Assocation on courses which put a premium on accurate driving.
- Unlike the other majors there is no immediate play-off if two players are tied for first place: they play a fifth 18-hole round the following day.
- Four players have won the Open four times: Willie Anderson, Bobby Jones, Ben Hogan and Jack Nicklaus.
- The oldest winner (in 1990) was Hale Irwin, at the age of 45; the youngest (in 1911) was John McDermott, aged 19.

**The British Open, July** – Or, again, just the Open to the home country. First held in 1860, it's run by the R&A, an offshoot of the Royal & Ancient Golf Club of St Andrews, and it's always played on a links course in Scotland or England.
- The Open is held at the St Andrews Old Course every five years.
- Its trophy is known as The Claret Jug.
- Harry Vardon holds the record for most Open victories, with six between 1896 and 1914.

**PGA Championship, August** – Hosted by the Professional Golfers' Association of America. It was originally a match play event, but changed to stroke play in 1958.
- Because it's the last major of the season it's known as 'Glory's Last Shot'.
- The biggest winning margins were by Paul Runyan (match play; 8 and 7; 1938) and Jack Nicklaus (stroke play; 7 strokes; 1980).

**And a few other men's events...**
- There are around twenty professional golf tours, such as the PGA Tour, the PGA European Tour, the Japan Golf Tour and the Asian Tour.
- The World Golf Championships are four annual events for professionals, one of them featuring match play and the others stroke play.
- There are several senior tours for men 50 and older.
- The Ryder Cup (*see page 140*) pitches the USA against Europe in match play. The Walker Cup is its amateur equivalent.

THWACK!

The wretched caddie hadn't told him it was possible to miss the hole from two feet.

# CHAPTER SIX

# BLAME THE CADDIE

If toting a heavy bag of clubs from hole to hole is becoming too much of a chore, perhaps you should consider hiring yourself a caddie. Sure, you'll need to visit the posh kind of club which provides the service, but you'll get much more than a pack-horse for your money – not least a raft of insider knowledge about the course and (with a handsome tip in view) an endless stream of friendly encouragement.

Better still, though, you'll have someone to blame when that hook shot lands in the water. Why on earth weren't you advised to use a different iron? Blame the caddie!

The first caddie on record was Andrew Dickson, who as a boy carried out the service for the Duke of York in his 'international' match on the Leith links in 1681 (*page 19*).

Thought to derive from the French 'cadet' – the youngest in a family – the word was used by the Scots to describe a general porter or errand boy long before it narrowed to today's specialised job description in the world of golf.

## A low blow

Pity James Parker, who once caddied for the actor Michael Douglas and three of his golfing friends. Walking ahead, he turned to face the following players and was struck low down in the most painful area of all. As a result, the poor man lost one of his testicles.

Serving a lawsuit on Douglas in 1999, Parker claimed that the actor had stuffed $60 into his back pocket when he saw him doubled up in pain. Douglas countered that someone else had hit the ball – and the case was later settled out of court.

## Double trouble

The most glaring example of caddie error in modern times cost the Welshman Ian Woosnam more than £200,000 at the 2001 British Open.

Playing the short first hole during the final round at Royal Lytham and St Anne's, 'Woosie' hadn't needed his driver. Now he arrived at the teeing box for the second hole, took the bag from his caddie, Myles Byrne, and met with a very nasty surprise indeed – he was carrying *two* drivers. He had been practising with them both the previous evening, and Byrne had failed to discard the one surplus to requirements. This meant that he had taken 15 clubs onto the course instead of the regulation 14.

The outcome was unavoidable: a two-stroke penalty. Woosnam, who later said the mistake had been on his mind throughout the round, would have finished second without the deduction – earning £360,000 instead of a 'mere' £141,666.

Byrne managed to keep his job ('He' won't do it again,' Woosnam said. 'I'm not going to sack him'), but only for a couple of weeks. He then committed another cardinal caddying sin by arriving late for a tournament in Sweden after a merry night out, and Woosnam had to break into a locker to retrieve his golfing shoes.

A newspaper headline said it all: 'Woosie sacks caddie who can't count or tell time!'

*Was there something in the Swedish air? At that same tournament the South African player Desvonde Botes arrived to find that his clubs had been stolen. His caddie had left the bag on the clubhouse verandah the previous evening!*

> 'Real golfers, no matter what the provocation, never strike a caddie with the driver. The sand wedge is far more effective.'
> – Huxtable Pippey

# Keeping busy

Here's a check-list of what a caddie is expected to do for a professional golfer:

- Walk the course in front of the player, carrying the bag. (It weighs about 20 kg / lbs, and has to be picked up some 50 times a round.)

- Give advice about the course, the weather and which clubs to use.

- Calculate the distance from various hazards and the greens. (Most use laser range finders these days.)

- Help 'read the greens' – that is, discuss the contours and the likely speed and turn of the ball – but without physically affecting play.

- Rake the sand in bunkers.

- Clean the ball (all caddies carry towels), repair any ball marks and attend the flag, but only if asked – the rules are strict.

- Give moral support if necessary – as it probably will be.

- Look after the player's physical well-being, from producing bananas to rubbing liniment into aching joints.

- Know the rules. In a tight spot he might be asked to recite them.

- Take care not to get hit by the ball: a player is penalised for hitting his own caddie, but not, for some reason, if he strikes someone else's.

## Seve's apple

Seve Ballesteros was known to be a hard taskmaster, but at the height of his success it was always easy for him to find a replacement whenever he fired his latest bag man. One of them, Ian Wright, later said, 'I knew he had a reputation for eating caddies for breakfast, and I was warned I'd get the blame for everything.' He was right!

During a 1989 Ryder Cup match at the Belfry in Warwickshire Wright advised the Spaniard to use a four iron rather than a three but was overruled. After Ballesteros had blazed the ball into a lake he reportedly told Wright, 'Make sure you get the yardage right on this one, because it will be the first you've got right all day.'

He lost the match, and Wright exploded in the dessing room, hurling the golfer's bag against the wall.

Another caddie, Joey Jones, took Ballesteros to court for loss of earnings after being sacked just six weeks into his contract (the case was dismissed), while Martin Gray – who, perhaps surprisingly, lasted for more than a year – fell out with his employer on the sixth hole of the Spanish Open in 1997 and the two agreed to separate there and then.

Gray had already had his patience tried at a tournament in Dubai, when the golfer complained about the hardness of an apple the caddie had given him. 'I don't know whether he wants a caddie or a greengrocer,' Gray commented.

## Pink on the greens

In 2005 an enterprising British firm, Eye Candy Caddies, launched a service offering attractive young women as caddies, using the slogan 'Golf made gorgeous'.

The girls were all properly trained, but the sight of them parading in their tight-fitting pink uniforms was too much for some traditionalists. One of the country's largest golf firms banned the company from its courses, complaining that the service was 'culturally insensitive' and would damage the reputation of the sport.

## An eccentric industrialist

The American billionaire John D. Rockefeller (1839–1937) didn't pick up a golf club until shortly before his sixtieth birthday, but once he'd got the bug he tackled the sport with all the determination that had inspired his success in business.

He created his own golf course, and then bought another which was immediately reduced to a membership of one – himself. He practised endlessly, playing golf almost every day for the rest of his life, and had time-and-motion films made of his swing.

> 'No game designed to be played with the aid of personal servants by right-handed men who can't even bring along their dogs can be entirely good for the soul.'
> – Bruce McCall

He was extremely demanding of his caddies, each of whom had to undertake specific, limited duties:

- One was employed solely to say 'Mr Rockefeller, keep your head down' whenever he addressed the ball.
- Another had the strange task of hammering a length of wood into the ground next to his employer's foot so that he wouldn't twist his left ankle (a persistent problem) when he shaped to swing.
- A third would push his bicycle, as in his later years he found walking the course too onerous.
- A fourth carried a thermos flask containing a home-made brew of milk and barley, which supposedly gave Rockefeller extra energy.

## Honour where it's due

For every player treating a caddie as a servant, another has demonstrated respect and even, at times, affection. When Walter Hagen won his first Open in 1922 he gave the cheque to his bag man – partly to demonstrate to the British authorities how mean their prize was, but also because (like many champions) he had been a caddie himself in his early years and had a proper estimation of the job.

Tom Watson took the lead in the 2003 US Open with his long-time caddy Bruce Edwards at his side. Edwards had been diagnosed with Lou Gehrig's disease (he would die in 2004), and Watson devoted both time and money during the year to helping Bruce raise money for motor neuron disease.

And when the veteran Lee Trevino flew in to St Andrews for the four-hole Champions Challenge in 2010 he asked the legendary Scottish caddie Willie Aitchison – now in his eighties – to walk the course with him, even though he had his own son as his assistant.

## A child caddie

Possibly the most enduring relationship between a golfer and his caddie began at the 1913 US Open in Brookline, Massachusetts. That was the year the local 20-year-old amateur Francis Ouimet beat two of the world's leading players (the Britons Harry Vardon and Ted Ray) in a play-off– with the 10-year-old Edward Lowery as his caddie. It was a victory which stimulated the spread of golf throughout the United States.

While Ouimet went on to further success as an amateur (in 1951, he became the first American to be elected captain of the Royal & Ancient at St Andrews), Lowery grew up to become a multi-millionaire car dealer. The two remained close friends though, and Lowery was a pall-bearer at Ouimet's funeral in 1967.

The story of the Open, and the young caddy's role in it, was told in the 2005 film '*The Greatest Game Ever Played*', with Josh Flitter playing Lowery.

## Beasts of burden

The caddy's role has been increasingly threatened by the spread of golf carts, especially in America. No, you don't get the professional advice, but you can travel with your clubs without having to bother about the weight.

In 2009 the golf cart itself met new competition at two clubs in North Carolina. They introduced llamas to do the carrying, each animal having a harness capable of holding two sets of clubs. The attraction? They have a calm temperament, they're cheap to feed and their padded feet don't damage the course.

# This working life

Most caddies begin as trainees at a golf club and will be promoted through the ranks if they show promise – an apprenticeship which can take ten years before they reach the top.

Usually they are paid at the end of a round in cash, although at some clubs they receive a ticket with which they can redeem their wages at the clubhouse. On top of the fees they can expect a tip from the players they've serviced – a percentage much in line with the rate a waiter would get in a restaurant.

At the top levels of professional golf a caddie hired full time will negotiate a deal which brings in a basic wage plus an agreed percentage of the player's winnings – which means that the best caddies can themselves make a good living from the job. As freelances, however, they are always vulnerable to falling out with the star who employs them.

Some are happy to remain caddies for the rest of their working lives, but a few have made the breakthrough into playing tournament golf themselves: Ben Hogan, Byron Nelson and Sam Snead are three big names who had that relatively humble start to their careers.

## The hippy bag man

The top caddies in professional golf not only earn big money but can become celebrities in their own right. Mike 'Fluff' Cowan, born in 1948, has worked for golfers such as Peter Jacobsen, Fred Couples and Jim Furyk, but most notably he was the bag man and adviser for the young Tiger Woods when he first catapulted onto the world scene.

An unkempt figure, sporting a large, white handlebar moustache, Cowan is often referred to as a hippy, and he proudly declares himself a fan of the rock band The Grateful Dead – a most unusual figure in a sport which tends to the prim and proper.

When he split up with Woods in 1999 there was speculation that the golfer had become uneasy about his caddy taking the limelight, because Cowan was by now himself attracting endorsements and appearing on TV commercials.

'The actual job hasn't changed' he said once. 'The biggest difference is that caddies today can actually make a living at it. It's become more of a business – a dedicated caddie with a top-notch player can make serious money.'

## The basics

We'll give the last word here to another celebrity caddie, the blonde and stocky Swede Fanny Sunesson. She worked with Nick Faldo for all of ten years, earning a reputed million pounds in combined wages and prize money.

In 1999, with Faldo's game on the wane, she decided it was time to find a more lucrative outlet – at first carrying the bag for the up-and-coming Spanish teenager Sergio Garcia.

Asked the secret of her success, she gave wannabee caddies three brief pieces of advice:

- **Never be late.**
- **Keep fit.**
- **Keep your mouth shut.**

# A beginner's guide to golf: 10. Laws of the green

Here are a few (severely simplified) rules relating to the putting green:

- You may remove 'loose impediments' but mustn't press anything down.

- If the ball is lifted (for cleaning, perhaps), its position must first be marked.

- You're allowed to repair an old hole plug or any damage previously caused by a ball.

- You're not allowed to test the surface of the green by scraping the surface or rolling a ball across it.

- You mustn't make a stroke 'from a stance astride, or with either foot touching, the line of putt'.

- You mustn't hit your ball while another one is on the move.

- If any part of your ball overhangs the lip of the hole you should approach it 'without unreasonable delay' and you're then allowed ten seconds to determine whether it's 'at rest'. If it drops in after that you add a stroke to your score.

# The Ryder Cup

The first Ryder Cup match between the US and Great Britain was held at Worcester Country Club, Massachusetts, in 1927. There had been unofficial matches between the two countries before, but the English entrepreneur Samuel Ryder, who'd made a fortune from selling seeds in penny packets, presented a cup for what he hoped would become a regular event.

He had his wish, although the tournament eventually became so hopelessly one-sided (yes, of course it was the Americans who kept on winning) that in 1979 it was decided to make it a US versus Europe event – and so it has been ever since.

The three-day tournament is held every two years, the venue usually alternating between America and the UK. Twelve players in each team are shuffled by their captains in a series of match play competitions, including foursomes, fourballs and singles.

Overall the two sides have been evenly matched. There were ties in 1969 and 1989, and Europe managed a hat-trick of victories from 2002–2006 although none of its players had won major championships during that period.

Cross-Atlantic relationships, unfortunately, have not always been harmonious:

• In 1991 there were furious exchanges between Seve Ballesteros and Paul Azinger, each accusing the other of cheating. At least this animosity led to what many felt was the best pairs match in history, Ballesteros and Olazábal beating Azinger and Beck 2 & 1.

• There was more unpleasantness in 1999 when the American Justin Leonard holed an incredible 45ft putt for a birdie at the 17th and other US players and some of their home crowd ran onto the green to celebrate – despite the fact that the European player, Olazábal, was still waiting to play his stroke.

No rules were broken, but the game's unwritten code of decorum certainly had been, and several of the Americans later apologised.

But a better spirit has sometimes prevailed:

• The US were the holders when they visited Royal Birkdale in 1969, and so needed only a tie to retain the trophy. There were squabbles between the players this time, too, but on the last green, with Tony Jacklin's ball two feet from the hole, Jack Nicklaus conceded the putt, and the tie – his 'gimme' regarded as one of the most outstanding examples of sportsmanship in golf.

S andra assured them that she thought her ball needed cleaning.

# CHAPTER SEVEN

# A CHAPTER OF ACCIDENTS

**A**nyone who has ever swung a golf club in earnest will testify to the malign influence of those fickle gods of the greens and fairways whose cruel reward for every fleeting stroke of genius is a chastening catalogue of disasters.

The fortunate may escape with nothing more than the embarrassment of fluffed shots and a score card in triple figures, but greater dangers still await the unwary, including injuries of various descriptions and (rather too often) death on the course.

Stern moralisers keen to point out personal failings should understand that there *is* such a thing as pure bad luck. Take the case of the Irishman, Harry Bradshaw, playing in the Open at Sandwich in 1949.

At the fifth hole he hit his tee shot into the semi-rough, discovering when he arrived that his ball was nestling inside the glass of a broken beer bottle.

'Had the rules been clear-cut,' he said later, 'I would have lifted and dropped, even at the expense of a penalty shot.'

What he did was shut his eyes and thwack the bottle with his driver. The glass shattered, and the ball travelled a paltry 30 yards. Bradshaw double-bogeyed the hole, which probably lost him the championship. He went on to defeat in a play-off at the hands of Bobby Locke.

Walter Hagen, or so the story goes, once found his ball caught up in a paper bag, the rules forbidding him to untangle it. He took a box of matches from his pocket (Hagen was a smoker) and simply set fire to the bag.

There was no such simple solution for Percy Alliss, playing for Great Britain against Gene Sarazen in the Ryder Cup in 1937.

Alliss had already reached the green when the American played a wayward shot which landed in the lap of a female spectator. She immediately jumped up and flicked the ball from her skirt – not only close to the hole, but blocking Alliss's approach.

By the rules of the time, the Englishman was 'stymied'. He wasn't allowed to move his opponent's ball, and he went down in three to Sarazen's two – eventually, to rub salt into the wound, losing the match by a single hole.

> **'Man blames fate for other accidents but feels personally responsible for a hole in one.'**
> **– Martha Beckman**

## A hole in ten

Sometimes, of course, it's just one of those days. A golfer can't blame anyone else, the weather or his clubs – he's simply playing more badly than he can ever remember. That's how it was for the Australian Bruce Devlin at the Andy Williams San Diego Open Invitational in 1975.

Devlin never won a major, his best position being fourth, but he was certainly much better than a casual spectator would have imagined seeing him hitting his ball into the water time and time again that day in front of the green on the 72nd hole (the very last in four long rounds of 18). He finally went down in... 10! A similarly dreadful 72nd hole experience befell the Frenchman Jean Van de Velde, who needed nothing more than a double-bogey six to win the British Open at Carnoustie in 1999.

Water was the problem here, too, Van de Velde pitching his ball into Barry Burn. After rolling up his trouser legs and climbing in, he took a penalty drop and then hit his ball into a bunker. Somehow he managed to shoot a triple-bogey seven, tying with two other players and then losing the play-off.

Let's provide some cheer to average golfers everywhere by giving a few other examples of disasters at the Open.

- Having made a red-faced 13 at the 13th hole in the Masters earlier that year, the Japanese player Tommy Nakajima needed five swings to dig himself out of the 6 ft-deep Road Hole bunker on the 17th hole of the Old Course at St Andrews in 1978. The media immediately named the hazard 'The Sands of Nakajima'.

- The German amateur Herman Tissies took all of 15 strokes to complete the par-three eighth hole (the Postage Stamp) at Troon in 1950. Three of them deposited the ball into a bunker; another five shots dug it out, but straight into another bunker; another two hoisted into a third bunker; two more strokes at last got the ball onto flat ground; and Tissies then needed three putts to hole out.

- The Australian Ian Baker-Finch had won the open four years earlier, but in 1995 he managed to miss the generously wide fairway from the first tee at St Andrews. In the same tournament he also pulled one ball into a hotel on his left and sliced another into a refreshment tent on his right.

# Limping to victory

Having half an inch cut off your leg to improve your golf might be regarded as excessive, but that's what Douglas Bader did.

It's true that the British flying ace of the second world war had 'tin' legs – losing them in an accident in 1931, but rejoining the RAF in 1939 to become one of its most renowned Spitfire and Hurricane pilots. Nonetheless, it was a bold move to have one of them permanently shortened.

Bader had been a brilliant sportsman before his accident, and after the war he took up golf with similar success. One of his friends, the golf writer Henry Longhurst (no mean amateur performer himself), noticed that Bader hit the ball best when playing on fairways that sloped uphill. The solution was obvious: shave a piece off one leg and he would always have a good 'lie'.

Why include this story in a chapter of accidents? Well, when Longhurst duly wrote an article about it Bader told him that he'd made a silly mistake – it wasn't his left peg that he'd asked to be trimmed, but his right.

'Good God,' Longhurst exploded, 'you've taken half an inch off the wrong leg!'

**D**ouglas Bader – the flying ace who had a leg shortened to improve his golf.

## One in the eye

Course managers everywhere must have shaken in their golfing shoes in 1999, when a Scottish golfer not only took Westhill Golf Club to court after losing an eye while playing there, but also named the head greenkeeper Dougal Duguid as responsible. Poor Muriel Milne already had only one-sixth vision in her right eye before her ball struck a stone inthe rough, shot up into her face and blinded the other one.

## What a stupid!

Although the Argentinian Roberto de Vicenzo won only one of the majors, the British Open in 1967, he might have added the Masters the following year but for a moment's carelessness.

When he made a birdie at the par 4 17th hole, his playing partner inadvertently entered a 4 instead of a 3 on his scorecard. De Vicenzo failed to check the card, and golf rules didn't allow a later correction. The proper score would have put him into a play-off for the championship.

'What a stupid I am!' he said afterwards.

Dreadful — but was it someone's fault or nothing more than an accident? Milne claimed that Duguid had been negligent, and she therefore claimed substantial damages.

In the event she lost her case, but several golf clubs elsewhere have found themselves footing the bill for injuries which common sense might dictate were just 'one of those things'.

Who's responsible, for instance, if someone wanders onto a golf course without being a paying customer and is then hit by a ball? A Turkish sailor who suffered that misfortune at Greenore, Ireland, in 1998 was technically trespassing, but after a wayward tee shot blinded him in one eye he successfully sued the club for more than 300,000 Euros.

The clumsy golfer himself was fortunately covered by his house insurance, but after this incident all clubs in Ireland rushed to take out policies. Two British court rulings suggest that it's a good idea for anyone who swings a club to do the same.

In the 1998 case of **Pearson v Lightning**, in the English Court of Appeal, the defendant had played a difficult shot from the rough which bounced off a tree and hit the plaintiff in the eye. No, of course he hadn't meant to do it – he had even yelled 'fore' when the ball careered towards his victim – but the judge ruled that the danger was 'foreseeable' and that he was therefore liable.

The errant golfer invoved in **Lewis v Buckpool Golf Club and Shipley**, at Elgin Sheriff Court in Scotland in 1993, was a poor and occasional player who had been given a 24 handicap for the purposes of an afternoon competition. His tee shot had careered off the 'toe' of the driver at an angle of 30 degrees.

His lack of talent, unfortunately, only increased the damages awarded against him. The sheriff ruled that the dreadful shot he had struck was 'not a mere possibility' or even a risk 'so small that in the circumstances a reasonable man would have been justified in disregarding it'. On the contrary, 'it was a real risk, and the worse the golfer, the greater the risk'.

## Deadly hazards

The victims in these cases suffered injury, but a worse fate has befallen an unlucky few. The first known accidental death in the sport was recorded in 1632 – not on a golf course, but in a churchyard at Fife, Scotland, where a man received 'ane deidle straik with ane golf ball... under his left lug'. Here are a few more sobering incidents:

- In 1963 a Canadian golfer, Harold Kalles, was attempting to play his ball out of a bunker when the shaft of his club broke against a tree. It cut his throat, and he died six days later.

- In 1993 another Canadian, Richard McCulough, lost his temper after making a poor tee shot at the 13th hole. He smashed his driver so violently against a golf cart that the head and six inches of the shaft flew through the air and struck his throat: he died in hospital later.

- In 1964 Tottenham Hotspur's brilliant Scottish international footballer John White, 27 years old and in his prime, was killed by lightning while sheltering under a tree in a thunderstorm at the Crews Hill course at Enfield in London.

- In 1991 a spectator, Bill Fadell, was killed and five were injured by lightning after taking shelter under a weeping willow during the US Open at Hazeltine National Golf Club in Minnesota.

Compared with these extreme examples of bad luck on the course, the future king of England got away lightly when a friend's club smacked him on the forehead, just above his left eye.

'We were on the putting green,' Prince William explained, 'and the next thing you know there was a seven-iron, and it came out of nowhere and it hit me in the head.'

The accident left the prince with what he refers to as a Harry Potter scar: 'I call it that because it glows sometimes, and some people notice it.'

> **'If you think it's hard to meet new people, try picking up the wrong golf ball.'**
> **– Jack Lemmon**

# Missing the fairway

'Laddie' Lucas, who would later represent Britain at golf in the Walker Cup, was a charismatic second world war fighter pilot.

When the engine of his Spitfire was hit by enemy fire over the Channel in 1944, he glided inland over the Prince's Club at Sandwich, which had been founded by his father and where he had often played.

After landing his machine belly-up in the rough by the ninth hole, Lucas commented dryly: 'I never could hit that fairway.'

# forms of address

In 1927 a Scottish court heard that a woman golfer hit another while giving a demonstration swing at an imaginary ball, allegedly having failed to address the ball first. This led to a misunderstanding in court.

Mr O'Connor (for the plaintiff): 'It is suggested that Miss Oldham spoke to an imaginary ball.'

Mr Justice Swift: 'You do not speak to the ball before you drive. You are thinking of addressing a jury, which is one thing; addressing a golf ball is another.'

The organisers were more than a little suspicious of the last-minute entrant.

# CHAPTER EIGHT

# BAD MANNERS

**N**o sport is more proud of its good breeding than golf, its aristocratic origins reflected in a strenuous emphasis on dress codes and etiquette, its meticulously detailed rule book designed to ensure fair play in every conceivable situation.

This, of course, throws into especially stark relief any sorry fall from grace. A display of bad temper on the links is as shocking to a purist as hearing an obscenity in the pulpit, while any trace of cheating condemns the wretched sinner to instant golfing oblivion.

# Illegal substances

Golf has suffered far fewer scandals than other big-money sports, but in 2007 the great Gary Player claimed that professional tournament players were abusing drugs on the circuit.

You may wonder what substances a golfer can possibly need while strolling around his comfortable green acres and occasionally wielding a club, but anything which gives overall strength for driving and steadies nerves for putting must be a temptation.

The initial response by the PGA was typically aloof: there was no evidence of drug abuse in the sport, and it didn't want its saintly players lumped in with the likes of 'footballers, basketball players and hockey players'.

> **"If there is any larceny in a man, golf will bring it out."**
> **– Paul Gallico**

However, the head of the World Anti-Doping Agency, Dick Pound, strongly urged the introduction of rigorous checks, adding, 'Golf is a game that has always prided itself on honesty, and testing would be a way of demonstrating that what you say is true.'

The PGA soon changed its stance, and the R&A's chief executive, Peter Dawson, also threw his weight behind the idea – while stressing that he had seen no evidence of any wrong-doing. *Golf was about to catch up with the rest of the sporting world.*

## Dirty cheats

For every suggestion of cheating in the professional game – and there have been very few of them – there are several examples of fair play being taken to the extremes.

Take the case of the Englishman Brian Davis, who in April 2010 was engaged in a play-off for the Verizon Heritage title in South Carolina. In playing his ball out of the rough at the 18th he was aware that his club had faintly touched a reed during his backswing.

There wasn't the slightest advantage to him in this, and nobody else had been aware of it, but the action broke Rule 13–4, because the reed counted as a 'loose impediment' which shouldn't be moved.

Although confessing cost him a two-stroke penalty, the tournament and more than $400,000, Davis remarked afterwards, 'I could not have lived with myself if I had not'.

Does that mean cheating is rare in golf as a whole? Not a bit of it! It's alive and sadly flourishing in the amateur game, as anyone who has ever fallen victim to it will (bitterly) tell you. On greens and fairways up and down the land there are fallible mortals who will stop at nothing in order to enter the clubhouse with a smile of victory on their faces.

How you cope with this unsporting behaviour will depend upon the state of your friendship and the importance of the result. As for tantrums, they will probably affect his game more than yours, so you can (embarrassing though it may be) let him get on with it.

# Cheats of the trade

- **The lost ball mysteriously discovered** – in a brilliant 'lie'. Your opponent is carrying a spare ball, possibly in a pocket with a convenient hole in it.

- **The nudged ball** – He (or she, of course) gets to his ball before you arrive and seems to be looking down at it, while firmly edging it forward with his shoe.

- **The unreliable marker** – He lifts his ball from the green for cleaning, putting his marker a little closer to the hole – and then, similarly, replaces the ball a little further hole-side of the marker.

- **The terrible mathematician** – In a friendly game you may not be paying close attention, but surely he needed seven strokes rather than five, didn't he? Check his card carefully next time.

- **The doubtful drop** – Your opponent asks for a free drop (not incurring a stroke) because of an obstacle in his way. You need to know the rules before refusing. Either way, make sure the drop is in the right place.

- **The fake handicap** – He manages to shave ten strokes off it, and then tries to kid you that he's simply having an uncharacteristic spurt of good form today.

- **Gamesmanship** – Questioning everything, swinging an arm to take his cap off as you drive, coughing loudly as you're about to putt – he knows just how to make you feel uneasy.

## Terrible Tommy

While most players would be frowned on for accepting defeat less than graciously, Tommy Bolt (1916–2008) made bad behaviour an intrinsic part of his on-course personality.

He won the US Open in 1958 and recorded 15 victories on the PGA Tour, but 'Terrible Tommy' or 'Thunder' became best known for his fiery temper.

'Always throw clubs ahead of you,' he once advised the young Arnold Palmer. 'That way you won't waste any energy going back to pick them up.'

> **'Golf is a game in which you yell "fore!", shoot six and write down five.'**
> **– Paul Harvey**

Perhaps the anger became pure showmanship in the end, as he once suggested – in 1969 he wrote a book with the ironic title *How to Keep Your Temper on the Golf Course* – but Ben Hogan, who helped coach him, thought he would have been a great player, rather than just a very good one, without all those histrionics.

Bolt was an exception who proved the rule. Not only was he popular on the circuit, but four years after his death he was voted into the World Golf Hall of Fame.

## Daly doses

One of the most colourful characters in modern golf is the American John Daly, who has fought a long battle against alcoholism.

At one time he had a reputation for quirky behaviour – walking off the course half way through a tournament, punching a spectator or losing his temper near the end of a round and hitting multiple balls into the water.

Despite his eccentricity, Daly has remained a popular figure on the circuit, suggesting that the sport perhaps isn't quite so stuffy after all.

## A little too open

There wasn't a trace of bad behaviour from the unknown Walter Danecki of Milwaukee when he took part in the Open at St Andrews in 1965. Whereas Tommy Bolt would throw a club after a bad shot, the dogged Walter kept smiling through despite posting mammoth scores of 108 and 113 in the qualifying rounds.

He fell short of the required score to take part in the tournament proper by a full 75 strokes. It turned out that the 43-year-old postal worker was a self-taught golfer who had played no more than a few casual rounds over his local course during the previous seven years. He couldn't easily join the PGA back home, so he thought a win at the British Open would set him on the road to stardom.

Two sizes of balls were allowed in those days, and Danecki had opted for the British one. 'Your small ball is right for this sort of course,' he said. 'If I had been playing our bigger ball I would have been all over the place.'

## It's that man again!

The R&A, shocked by this unbecoming behaviour, were determined that nothing so outrageous should ever again sully the reputation of the Open – but they had reckoned without Maurice Flitcroft.

In 1976 this 46-year-old, chain-smoking shipyard crane operator from Barrow-in-Furness, a man who had never played 18 holes in his life, who had taken up the sport only 18 months before and had practised for the Open by driving balls on his local beach and putting into buried coffee tins in his back garden, was somehow accepted for the qualifying rounds.

He began with an 11 and a 12 (officially: his marker admitted to losing count), managed par just once among a string of triple and quadruple bogeys, and posted a score of 121 – a record 49 over par which still stands.

Flitcroft withdrew, and the organisers must have believed they had seen the last of him. Some hopes! He was to plague them for years to come.

He was rumbled when posing as Arnold Palmtree and Count Manfred von Hoffmenstal, but on three occasions – despite being banned for life by the unamused R&A – he managed to tee-off once again for the greatest prize in British golf.

In 1978, presumably in tribute to his predecessor Walter Danecki, he was the American Gene Pacecki ('as in pay cheque,' he explained when handing in his form), and he survived a few holes before being ejected.

In 1984 he dyed his hair and wore a false moustache to become Gerald Hoppy, a pro from Switzerland who went round the first nine holes in 63. As he said afterwards, they must have thought they had another Maurice Flitcroft on their hands: 'Imagine their surprise when they discovered they had the actual Maurice Flitcroft on their hands!'

He was back again in 1990 as James Beau Jolley, but was turfed out before he could complete the third hole.

'I never set out to belittle them,' he said afterwards in puzzlement. 'Golf's just a game, and I tried my best. What did they need to get so uptight about?'

James Thurber, the American writer and cartoonist who created that hopelessly aspiring character Walter Mitty, seems to have missed a trick in not including golf in his hero's repertoire. *Never mind: several of his fellow authors have made up for that unaccountable lapse...*

## Seeing a ghost

During the most cantankerous tournament in Ryder Cup history Britain's Lee Westwood accused the American favourite Boo Weekley of inciting the home crowds.

His reward was a stream of abuse from the locals – including a visitation from a ghost.

'The ghost was some guy with a white sheet over his head,' Westwood later reported. 'He jumped out at me and went "Boooooo!" in my face. He was the only one who got ejected, but he was the one that made me laugh.'

'**G**olf, like the measles, should be caught young, for, if postponed to riper years, the results may be serious.'

British author and passionate golfer
P.G. Wodehouse

# CHAPTER NINE

# LITERARY GOLFERS

I t's probably just as well that P.G. Wodehouse had a golf handicap of 18. After all, had he been any good at the game he might have taken it so seriously as to consider it an improper subject for his humour. As it was, he became the unofficial laureate of the links, basing dozens of his short stories on its power to enthrall, frustrate and enrage.

But many other writers have been hooked on the game, too. John Updike wrote that playing it produced 'a bliss that at times threatens to relegate all the rest of life... to the shadows.'

# Writers on golf

**G.K. Chesterton:** 'I regard golf as an expensive way of playing marbles.'

**H.L. Mencken:** 'If I had my way, any man guilty of golf would be barred from any public office in the United States and the families of the breed would be shipped off to the white slave corrals of Argentina.'

**A.A. Milne:** 'Golf is so popular simply because it is the best game in the world at which to be bad.'

**John Updike:** 'Golf appeals to the idiot in us and the child. Just how childlike golf players become is proven by their frequent inability to count past five.'

**H.G. Wells:** 'The uglier a man's legs are, the better he plays golf. It's almost a law.'

**William Wordsworth:** 'Golf is a day spent in a round of strenuous idleness.'

In the novel *Rabbit, Run* his character Harry 'Rabbit' Angstrom is on the golf course with Rev. Jack Eccles trying to explain what's missing in his life. Rabbit is useless at golf, but he suddenly manages to strike a perfect shot and cries out, 'That's it!' – he has known a rare moment of spiritual uplift.

And in his short story 'Farrell's Caddie', Updike has his Scottish caddie say, 'Ye kin tell a' aboot a man frae th' way he gowfs.'

## Is a golfer a gentleman?

The English humourist and novelist A.P. Herbert wrote a series of spoof legal reports for *Punch* magazine during the 1920s and 30s , all featuring Albert Haddock, a perpetutal defendant standing up for his civil liberties in the courts.

In 'Is a Golfer a Gentleman?' we learn that he has been summoned under the Profane Oaths Act 1745 for uttering swear words ('more than 400 in number') while trying to play his ball out of a deep coastal chasm on a course in Cornwall.

The penalties are greater for gentlemen, but Haddock argues that the trials of golf are so severe that a man should not be expected to behave as a gentleman while playing it.

The judge, agreeing with him, declares that otherwise respectable elderly gentlemen may be found all over the country hacking away at sandpits in a blind fury.

'It is clear,' he rules, 'that the game of golf may well be included in that category of intolerable provocations which may legally excuse or mitigate behaviour not otherwise excusable, and that under that provocation the reasonable or gentle man may reasonably act like a lunatic or lout respectively, and should legally be judged as such.'

> 'The reason the pro tells you to keep your head down is so you can't see him laughing.'
> – Phyllis Diller

# Sherlock Holmes returns

Sir Arthur Conan Doyle was such a keen golfer, belonging to several clubs and in 1910 becoming captain of his local one at Crowborough Beacon in Sussex, that it's surprising to find that none of his Sherlock Holmes tales is set on the links. In fact, a passing reference to a discussion about golf clubs in The Adventure of the Greek Interpreter is the only mention of the sport in all those novels.

Golf did, however, play a vital part in the return of Holmes several years after the author had killed him off – to huge public protest – at the Reichenbach Falls. In March 1901 Doyle spent a weekend with his friend Fletcher Robinson at the Royal Links Hotel in Cromer, Norfolk, and while they enjoyed a round of golf Robinson related to him a ghostly legend about a fearful beast said to haunt the moors around Dartmoor.

Despite Doyle's insistence that the detective was still dead, and that the story told in The Hound of the Baskervilles was an earlier case related by Dr Watson years later, he soon found himself writing a set of thirteen new Holmes stories.

## Shaken, not stirred

The writer Ian Fleming was a fervent player, and when he wrote a golf match into his 1959 James Bond novel Goldfinger (it was turned into a film in 1964) he thinly disguised his home club Royal St George's at Sandwich, Kent, as Royal St Mark's, and its pro Albert Whiting as Albert Blacking.

Being a dastardly crook, Auric Goldfinger of course cheats at golf, and Bond – in fiction's most celebrated golf match – has to play tricks of his own in order to beat him, switching his opponent's Dunlop 1 ball for a Dunlop 7 and using a Penfold Heart himself.

**What happened next:**

- Sean Connery, playing the Bond role in the film of Goldfinger, discovered a passion for the game.

- With the film still in production, Ian Fleming died of a heart attack at the age of 56 after a committee meeting at Royal St George's, where he was captain-elect.

- The Penfold Golf company in Birmingham was inundated with orders for Penfold Heart balls.

# A thousand lost balls

There's no record of the poet T.S. Eliot ever playing golf (whether across a wasteland or anywhere else), but in a literary chapter we must include his reference to the sport. In his poem 'The Rock' he imagines archaeologists of a future generation coming upon the traces of our own worthless society.

*And the wind shall say:*
*Here were decent godless people,*
*Their only monument the asphalt road*
*And a thousand lost golf balls.*

# A bad lie

Jordan Baker, one of the leading characters in F. Scott Fitzgerald's *The Great Gatsby*, is soon revealed to be shallow and untrustworthy. A professional golfer, she has been accused of moving her ball from a bad lie during the semi-final of her first big tournament.

The two witnesses to the incident, including a caddie, later change their minds – but the novel's narrator, Nick Carraway, has caught her out telling a lie, and her rumoured behaviour on the golf course helps convince him that she is 'incurably dishonest'.

# Ten Golf Novels

A batch of contemporary works of fiction which have golf as their background:

**A Wicked Slice**  Charlotte & Aaron Elkins

**Dead Solid Perfect**  Dan Jenkins

**Loopy: a novel of golf and Ireland**  Dan Binchy

**Miracle on the 17th Green**  James Patterson & Peter de Jonge

**Sudden Death**  Michael Balkind

**Take Dead Aim**  Don Wade

**The Caddie**  J. Michael Veron

**The Green**  Troon McAllister

**The Rub of the Green**  William Halberg

**Waggle**  Joe Redden Tigan

## The Oldest Member

And so back to P.G. 'Plum' Wodehouse, whose Oldest Member, 'snug in his favourite chair', appears in a stream of golfing short stories and novels.

This unnamed ancient, whose clubhouse perch overlooks the ninth hole, buttonholes anyone within hailing distance to dispense his invaluable wisdom and advice.

A typical Wodehouse story, 'A Woman is Only a Woman', tells of two friends, Peter Willard and James Todd, who fall in love with the same girl, the attractive Grace Forrester.

The Oldest Member, himself unmarried, admits to having little experience in such matters, but tells us, admiringly, that 'once, at a picnic, I observed her killing wasps with a teaspoon, and was impressed by the freedom of her back-swing'.

Peter and James, both exceedingly poor golfers, have been accustomed to playing long rounds together without any hint of animosity between them. Now they are aware of a friction – until they decide to play an 18-hole match after which the loser must disappear and leave the romantic field open to his rival.

During the match both of the men manage to speak to Grace alone, and both immediately decide that they don't want to marry her after all. Why? Because she's always regarded golf as 'a game for children with water on the brain who weren't athletic enough to play Kiss-in-the-ring'.

## The missing caddie

**Question**: Which 20th century American novel opens with a scene on a golf course?

**Answer**: William Faulkner's *The Sound and the Fury*.

The first part of the novel is 'a tale told by an idiot', Benjy, who is devastated when his beloved sister Caddy disappears from his life after a scandal. Benjy keeps revisiting the course because – or so it seems to him – he hears the golfers repeatedly calling out her name.

The two men shiver in sympathy, silently clasp hands and agree that they have had a lucky escape. For the Oldest Member the moral of the tale is clear: 'a woman is only a woman, but a hefty drive is a slosh'.

## Noisy butterflies

We'll leave the last word with Wodehouse, as he so well understood the frustrations, as well as the joys, of the game. In 'Ordeal by Golf' he tells the story of young Mitchell Holmes, a man with a fiery temper on the course.

Which golfer will not sympathise with this description?

*'He was the sort of player who does the first two holes in one under par and then takes an eleven at the third. The least thing upset him on the links. He missed short putts because of the uproar of the butterflies in the adjoining meadows...'*

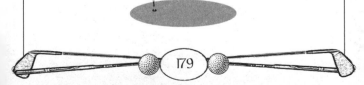

# Ten golf courses to play before you die

Of course you'll want to play at St Andrew's Old Course in Scotland, which is the very cradle of golf, and at Augusta National, which is the epitome of American lushness, but here are a few venues around the world with unusual, often challenging, features:

**Cypress Point, Pebble Beach, California** – This scenic wonder, designed by Alister Mackenzie, has a par-three 16th which demands that the ball is actually hit across the Pacific Ocean.

**Furnace Creek, Death Valley, California** – For contrast: the hottest golf course on earth, set in baking desert (so do take plenty of water with you).

**Cooper Pedy Opal Fields, Australia** – Another dry course, with no grass (you carry your own patch of turf), and so hot that it's best to play at night, using glowing balls.

**Valderrama, Cadiz, Spain** – Beautiful but tough, with two opposing winds to test your ability.

**San Lorenzo, The Algarve, Portugal** – This one's set in a nature reserve, so there's plenty of wildlife to distract you. Take special care on the 6th, which takes a dog-leg round a mountain on one side and has the banks of the Rio Formosa on the other.

**Estonian Golf and Country Club, Manniva Village, Estonia** – A bit of a secret, although it *is* on the PGA Tour. The long daylight hours mean you can play after midnight in June, using 'tracer' balls that flash when you hit them.

**The Legend Golf Resort, Entabenia Safari Park, South Africa** – Once you've been captivated by the scenery on this stunning course you can have a go at the 'extreme' 19th, a par-3 which you tackle by taking a helicopter to the tee half a kilometre above the hole and driving your ball into the chasm beyond. Then, of course, it's back into the helicopter to finish the hole.

**Couer d'Alene Resort, Idaho** – The 14th hole is billed as 'the world's only par-3 movable island green', which you reach by taking the special Putter Boat shuttle from the shore.

**Green Zone Golf Club, Lappi, Finland** – Eleven of the holes lie in Finland and the rest in Sweden. Teeing off at the 6th hole you're in a different time zone from the green, so that the ball travels through the air for more than an hour to complete a hole in one.

**Nullabor Links, South Australia** – It has the usual 18 holes, but the course stretches for all of 1,365 kilometres (848 miles), with an average distance between holes of 66 kilometres (41 miles). Take your time – and don't think about walking the course.

# Golf Timeline

**1457** Earliest known written record of golf being played in Scotland: a parliamentary ban on the playing of golf as it distracts young men who should be learning their archery skills.

**1470** Ban on golf affirmed.

**1491** Parliament reaffirms the golf ban.

**1502** The ban is lifted after Scotland and England sign the Treaty of Glasgow. James IV buys a set of clubs from a Perth bow-maker.

**1552** First record of golf being played at St Andrews in Fife.

**1567** Mary, Queen of Scots is accused of playing golf soon after the murder of her husband, Lord Darnley.

**1592** Golf is banned in Edinburgh at the time of sermons on Sundays.

**1618** Invention of the 'featherie' ball of leather stuffed with feathers. James VI of Scotland and 1 of England confirms the right to play golf on Sundays.

**1636** David Wedderburn's Latin guide *Vocabula* includes a section on golf .

**1682** First recorded international match: the Scots beat the English at Leith.

**1724** First golf match reported in a British newspaper.

**1743** Thomas Mathieson's mock-heroic poem 'The Goff' is published.

**1744** First set of golf rules drawn up by the Company of Gentlemen Golfers, playing at Leith.

**1754** Royal & Ancient Golf Club founded. Silver cup awarded for an open championship on the Old Course.

**1759** Earliest reference to stroke, rather than match, play.

**1766** The Blackheath Club in London becomes the first golf club outside Scotland.

**1774** The first part-time golf professional is hired – by the Edinburgh Burgess Society.

**1786** The South Carolina Golf Club at Charleston in the USA becomes the first outside the United Kingdom.

**1810** The earliest recorded reference to a women's tournament at Musselburgh.

**1812** First mention of bunkers and putting greens in the rules of golf.

**1832** Foundation of the North Berwick Club in Scotland, which is the first to admit women – although they are not allowed to play in competitions.

**1833** Perth Golfing Society is the first to be granted the 'royal' prefix.

**1848** Invention of the gutta-percha ball (the 'guttie'), which is cheaper than the feathery and travels further.

**1858** A match is officially deemed as taking place over 18 holes.

**1867** The first golf club for women is founded – the Ladies' Golf Club at St Andrews.

**1889** The diameter of the hole is fixed at 4¼ in (10.8 cm), and its depth at least 4 in (10.16 cm).

**1890** The term 'bogey' is invented in the UK.

**1892** First 18-hole golf course in America, on a sheep farm in Downers Grove, Illinois. Gate money is charged for the first time at a match in Britain – between Douglas Rollard and Jack White at Cambridge.

**1895** The United States Open is founded.

**1897** The Royal & Ancient Golf Club (R&A) is recognised as the governing body for golf in Britain. Pool cues banned for putting in America.

**1898** The term 'birdie' is invented in the USA. The first rubber-cored ball, the Haskell, is patented by Coburn Haskell.

**1902** The first groove-faced irons are introduced.

**1903** The American Arthur F. Knight patents his Schenectady putter.

**1905** The first dimple-patterned golf balls are patented by William Taylor in England.

**1910** Arthur F. Knight patents steel shafts.

**1920** Britain and the United States agree that a ball should be no heavier than 1.62 ounces (45.9 gm) and no less than 1.62 in (4.11 cm) in diameter.

**1922** First Walker Cup match.

**1925** First fairway irrigation system developed at Dallas, Texas.

**1926** First steel shafts made in the US (1929 in UK). Gate money is introduced at the British Open.

**1927** The inaugural Ryder Cup matches are played between the United States and Britain.

**1932** First Curtis Cup matches are held in England. Gene Sarazen introduces the sand-wedge.

**1934** First US Masters is played.

**1938** The permitted maximum number of clubs to be carried is fixed at 14 in the USA (1939 in UK).

**1952** The R&A and the United States Golf Association (USGA) establish a unified code of rules.

**1960** Lifting, cleaning, and repairing ballmarks is allowed on the putting green for the first time.

**1964** The first grandstands are built at the Open championships in Britain.

**1966** First live coverage of the British Open beamed to America.

**1973** The graphite shaft is invented.

**1974** The larger American ball of 1.68 in (4.3 cm) diameter becomes compulsory at the British Open.

**1979** The first metal drivers are introduced. The Ryder Cup is reorganised to become a tournament between the USA and Europe.

**1990** The R&A adopts the American ball, which becomes the standard in world golf.

# Glossary

**ace** The American term for a hole-in-one, a player's first shot carrying all the way from the tee into the hole.

**bagman** Another word for a caddie – a paid assistant who gives advice about which clubs to use and which sorts of shot to play.

**blackballing** A method of preventing people from joining a club by admitting members only by a secret vote – often involving racial prejudice in days gone by.

**hazard** An obstacle on the course, such as a bunker or a water feature, designed to create a difficulty.

**links** A golf course by the sea.

**mock-heroic poem** A humorous work which applies grand rhetoric to a lowly subject.

**open events** Tournaments in which both amateurs and professionals can compete.

**PGA** The Professional Golfers' Association of America, which hosts the annual PGA Championship.

**PGA Tour** A separate organisation which organises the main professional men's golf tours in the US and North America.

**R&A** An offshoot of the Royal & Ancient at St Andrews, the R&A is the governing body of golf for all the world bar the United States and Mexico.

**sand trap** A bunker.

**stymie** Until the rules were changed in 1952, a player was stymied if an opponent's ball lay between his own ball and the hole. He had to putt over or around it.

**sweet spot** The best part of the club with which to hit the ball.

**USGA** The equivalent of the R&A for the United States and Mexico.

# Index

# INDEX

**Name** *Gabriei N'Cherish*   **H'cap**   **Date**

Player's Signature

Marker's Signature

| Marker's Score | Hole | Yards | Par | Metres | Stroke Index | Player's Score | Won + Lost − Halved 0 |
|---|---|---|---|---|---|---|---|
| | 1 | 368 | 4 | 336 | 8 | 5 | |
| | 2 | 300 | 4 | 274 | 11 | 5 | |
| ● | 3 | 273 | 4 | 249 | 13 | 3 | |
| | 4 | 440 | 4 | 402 | 3 | 4 | |
| | 5 | 129 | 3 | 118 | 18 | 3 | |
| | 6 | 438 | 4 | 399 | 1 | 6 | |
| | 7 | 387 | 4 | 354 | 6 | 4 | |
| | 8 | 196 | 3 | 180 | 16 | 3 | |
| | 9 | 536 | 5 | 490 | 5 | 7 | |
| | Out | 3067 | 35 | 2802 | | 4 | |
| | 10 | 363 | 4 | 332 | 9 | 5 | |
| | 11 | 267 | 4 | 244 | 14 | 5 | |
| | 12 | 473 | 5 | 432 | 4 | 3 | |
| | 13 | 221 | 3 | 203 | 15 | 4 | |
| | 14 | 427 | 4 | 390 | 2 | 6 | |
| | 15 | 310 | 4 | 284 | 12 | 4 | |
| ● | 16 | 159 | 3 | 145 | 17 | 4 | 4 |
| | 17 | 391 | 4 | 357 | 10 | 4 | |
| | 18 | 478 | 5 | 437 | 7 | | |
| | In | 3089 | 36 | 2824 | | | |
| | Out | 3067 | 35 | 2802 | SSS | | |
| | Total | 6156 | 71 | 5626 | 69 | | |

Handicap

Net score